OXFORD BOOK OF
POETRY FOR CHILDREN

Compiled by

EDWARD BLISHEN

With illustrations by

BRIAN WILDSMITH

OXFORD UNIVERSITY PRESS

OXFORD   TORONTO   MELBOURNE

Oxford University Press, Walton Street, Oxford OX2 6DP

Oxford New York
Athens Auckland Bangkok Bogota Bombay
Buenos Aires Calcutta Cape Town Dar es Salaam
Delhi Florence Hong Kong Istanbul Karachi
Kuala Lumpur Madras Madrid Melbourne
Mexico City Nairobi Paris Singapore
Taipei Tokyo Toronto

and associated companies in
Berlin Ibadan

Oxford is a trade mark of Oxford University Press

ISBN 0 19 276031 9 (hardback)
0 19 276058 0 (paperback)

© Edward Blishen 1963
First published 1963
Reprinted 1984, 1985, 1986, 1988,1989, 1991, 1993, 1994
First published as paperback 1985
Reprinted 1987, 1989, 1991, 1993
Reissued with new cover 1996

Printed and bound in Hong Kong

CONTENTS

Collecting these poems was an alarming (though pleasant) task: putting them into order was terrifying (though very agreeable). – *Well*, you will say, *what can have frightened him?* – You have the answer if you think what I was to do. There was to be one book only: there were to be . . . I haven't actually counted the poems, but whatever the number is, it is a *limited* number. Imagine, those of you who collect things because they give you pleasure, having to choose for showing only a *small* selection of your shells, or birds' feathers, or fossils, or whatever they may be. There were – and this is important – thousands of poems I could and would have wished to put into this book: I have chosen, naturally, as well as I can (as you would with your shells); but a point about poetry (and no book must ever be allowed to suggest otherwise) is that there

INTRODUCTION

is a great richness and exciting quantity of it. This is a gathering, the gathering one collector might make on one beach on a single morning. I hope it will be found an enjoyable gathering – but I hope, too, that no one will suppose it is anything more. Behind each poem in this book are countless others, there for the looking: and my hope is that you will want to look for them – that this book, when it has done its work of giving pleasure, will go on to do its even more important work of making you impatient for more.

Of course, to know a few poems deeply is better than to know many poems in a quick vague way. It is a fact that when we are young poems affect us – stir us or touch us or amuse us or beautifully puzzle us – as they never quite do again. I remember when I was a small boy at school, each of us in our class made one poem his own; and we would stand out in turn, at the end of afternoons, to recite our poems. Even now, a long time later, I can hear *A Boy's Song* (which you will find on page 138), recited as it was by a small serious boy whose main idea about speaking verse was that you should go faster and faster as you went along: that last verse

> But this I know, I love to play
> Through the meadow among the hay;
> Up the water, and over the lea,
> That's the way for Billy and me.

went so swiftly that I had always a vision of Billy and the boy skimming the water and fleeting like larks across the lea: but also all the *pictures* in the poem – of the sleeping grey trout, the mowers mowing clean, the clustering nuts and the thick green hay – made one large picture: or rather, a world into which I entered, and that I could see and smell and touch. I can see and smell and touch it now – you have only to read me the poem, rather fast. My own special poem in those days was *The Pedlar's Caravan*, which you will find on page 145; I don't to this day know if it's a good poem or not – but I have only to let its words run through my head and I am back in that world of tin chimneys and brown babies and tea trays: one of the worlds created for me when I was young by poems.

Because I hope that among the poems in this book will be some that will give you, in this way, worlds to live in, scenes or feelings you will never forget, I have chosen them with care: and I mean I have chosen none that have not, to my knowledge, been makers of worlds and scenes and feelings to children somewhere or to myself when a child. I have been helped in this by my own sons, whom I would like to thank: and (in the past, long before I began this collection) by other children, especially in Islington – them, too, I would thank.

Arrangement was difficult. I could have put the easy poems first and followed them by more difficult poems: but looking at poems as "easy" or "difficult" doesn't seem very sensible. If you are seven, say, you may be able to read *As I was going up Pippin Hill* (on page 34) for yourself; you might find *The Forsaken Merman* full of words awkward to read and of things said in a difficult manner. But if someone read *The Forsaken Merman* (on page 59) aloud to you (and being read aloud is something that should happen to every poem), I think that "difficult" is not the word you would use of it. A poem simple in language and form can contain a difficult idea: a big poem with long words can say something quite

6

straightforward. So I didn't think the idea of a growing difficulty was one on which to base an arrangement. I turned then to the idea of dividing the poems into subjects: poems about the sea, about fairies, about people, about animals. Good poems don't easily drop into pockets like this: *The Golden Vanity*, on page 57, is about the sea but it is also about courage and cruelty. And even to say a poem is "about" this or that seems queer: rather like saying that a wood is about trees, or the sea itself is about water. This is, however, in the end, how I have arranged the book, preferring to do so rather than to pour my poems all over the place; but I have tried to keep some sense of uncertainty about my divisions by giving them titles that, like many poems themselves, are a little mysterious and not briskly particular or exact. For example, I could have given the title "People" to the little section that is indeed a group of poems about human beings of one kind or another: but I preferred to use the phrase "A Chip Hat Had She On", which is a sentence that gives me great pleasure and is, I think, as strange as it ought to be. But the truth is that these divisions are like the signposts and street names and informative policemen that help us to find our way about a strange town. In no time at all we don't need them. I hope you will find my titles and divisions just as useful – and no more. Don't take them too seriously.

I have one or two small practical things to say. The first is to tell anyone who may be puzzled that Anon, who wrote so many of the poems in this book, is many people: he is anonymous, the nameless poet who wrote our ballads, and many old songs, and little snatches of verse of one kind or another: and sometimes he isn't even a single poet, but a mass of people who have added to a poem, or taken away from it, or changed its words through the years as they have written it down or spoken it aloud. That is why, here and there, you may come across a poem that you know in a slightly different form. My second point is that there are one or two poems in this book containing words that those of us not born and bred in Scotland may never have seen before. To put it rather oddly, much of the best poetry in English is in Scotch; that is to say the language is plainly English, but with Scottish words here and there, or Scottish forms of English words. If I had left out these poems I should have been treating you as cowards, who were ready to run as soon as you saw a strange word; and worse still, I should have been assuming that you weren't able to love these words for their own sakes, fine to look at and finer to roll on your tongue as many of them are. And worse than all this, I should have been hiding from you the fact that there is a great deal of magnificent Scots verse, much of it story-telling verse, that I hope you will go on to read. To make things easier at a first reading, I have given at the foot of the Scots poems the meaning of words that might be really puzzling: but having read a meaning, I expect you will want to forget it. It is useful to know that the "skeely skipper" the king calls for in *Sir Patrick Spens* (page 47) is a "skilful" one: but once one knows that, then "skeely" becomes the right and only word for him. As for the "gurly" sea that overwhelms Sir Patrick and his lairds, it is necessary to be sure that our guess is right, and that "gurly" means "stormy"; but once we are certain of it, we know that "gurly" simply means "gurly", and that no other word whatever could take its place.

My last practical point is that (as I've already half-said, and now I say it fully) the true life and beauty of a poem is often felt only when it is spoken aloud. We do much silent reading now: if your father recited the newspaper at breakfast, or if your whole family read its books aloud as they sat round the fire of an evening, we might not be too pleased with the results. But much of the beauty and excitement of poetry lies in its sound: we *can* hear it in our heads, when we read silently, but what we hear is only a whisper of what we should be hearing. In a way, reading poetry silently is like reading music from a score: it can be done, and there are times when it must be done; but how much better it is to hear the orchestra – how much better it is to hear the poem.

A final word. Don't worry if there are poems in this book (or elsewhere) that you don't like. We have no duty to like a poem. And don't worry if here and there you find a poem you don't understand, in the sense that you couldn't give anyone a clear idea what it was "about". Words, lines, whole poems may come to us as mysteries. They may be mysteries that please us, that give us a strange deep feeling of this or that. That feeling may be our way of understanding a poem. *Four Ducks on a Pond* (on page 66) makes me feel deeply sad: I can't say exactly why. *The Owl*, page 65, gives me a feeling of deep delight: I can't say exactly why. Being unable to give reasons for the effect poems have on us is nothing to be worried about: understanding, in the usual meaning of the word, may come to us later, or it may never come; but this does not greatly matter – because understanding a poem may be something different from understanding, say, a story in a newspaper, or the directions on a bottle. Of course, we may understand very clearly indeed – as we appreciate without difficulty that in *The Snare* (on page 130) James Stephens is saying (surely he is saying?) that we should not be cruel to other living creatures. But a poem does not need to have this clear, definite meaning, any more than a magic spell does, or any more than does the feeling we have when we smell, say, autumn leaves, or lavender, or the salt on our skins when we come out of the sea. Indeed, one of the great joys of poetry (and I hope you will find it so) is that it satisfies not only our minds (which are usually well-fed else-where) but our hearts and the whole *feeling* part of us.

I have been solemn: so, as a truly last word, let me say that poetry is not always serious or mysterious, nor does it always stir in us grave emotions. Poetry, as I hope this collection will make clear, can laugh, chuckle, make jokes. The subject of poetry, in fact, may be anything whatever that can be expressed by human beings with a sense of words and of rhythm, a sharp eye, a keen ear, an inquiring mind and an open heart: and I hope this book, meant as a sort of introduction to the huge rich world of poetry, will be found to have within it many of the worlds, many of the feelings and scenes, many of the kinds of enchantment and amusement that poetry has to offer.

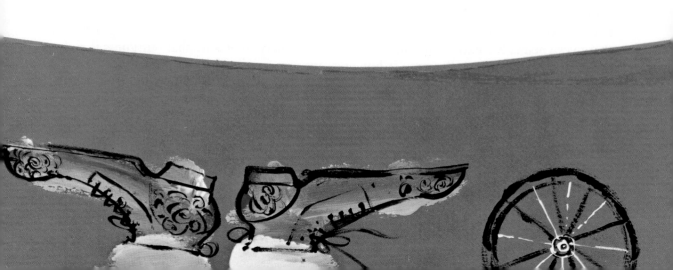

THE MOON'S IN A FIT

We're all in the dumps,
For diamonds are trumps,
The kittens are gone to Saint Paul's,
The babies are bit,
The moon's in a fit,
And the houses are built without walls.

Anon

10

AIKEN DRUM

There was a man lived in the moon,
  and his name was Aiken Drum.
And he played upon a ladle,
  and his name was Aiken Drum.

And his hat was made of good cream
                        cheese,
  and his name was Aiken Drum.
And he played upon a ladle,
  and his name was Aiken Drum.

And his coat was made of good roast beef,
  and his name was Aiken Drum.
And he played upon a ladle,
  and his name was Aiken Drum.

And his buttons were made of penny
                        loaves,
  and his name was Aiken Drum.
And he played upon a ladle,
  and his name was Aiken Drum.

His waistcoat was made of crust of pies,
  and his name was Aiken Drum.
And he played upon a ladle,
  and his name was Aiken Drum.

His breeches were made of haggis bags,
  and his name was Aiken Drum.
And he played upon a ladle,
  and his name was Aiken Drum.

There was a man in another town,
  and his name was Willy Wood.
And he played upon a razor,
  and his name was Willy Wood.

And he ate up all the good cream cheese,
  and his name was Willy Wood.
And he played upon a razor,
  and his name was Willy Wood.

And he ate up all the good roast beef,
  and his name was Willy Wood.
And he played upon a razor,
  and his name was Willy Wood.

And he ate up all the penny loaves,
  and his name was Willy Wood.
And he played upon a razor,
  and his name was Willy Wood.

And he ate up all the good pie crust,
  and his name was Willy Wood.
And he played upon a razor,
  and his name was Willy Wood.

But he choked upon the haggis bags,
  and there was an end of Willy Wood.
And he played upon a razor,
  and his name was Willy Wood.

                                        Anon

There was an old person of Dean
Who dined on one pea, and one bean;
    For he said, "More than that
    Would make me too fat,"
That cautious old person of Dean.
                    Edward Lear

Beautiful Soup, so rich and green,
  Waiting in a hot tureen!
Who for such dainties would not stoop?
Soup of the evening, beautiful Soup!
Soup of the evening, beautiful Soup!
  Beau-ootiful Soo-oop!
  Beau-ootiful Soo-oop!
Soo-oop of the e-e-evening,
  Beautiful, beautiful Soup!

Beautiful Soup! Who cares for fish,
  Game, or any other dish?
Who would not give all else for two p
ennyworth only of beautiful Soup?
Pennyworth only of beautiful Soup?
  Beau-ootiful Soo-oop!
  Beau-ootiful Soo-oop!
Soo-oop of the e-e-evening,
  Beautiful, beauti-FUL SOUP!

Lewis Carroll

CALICO PIE

Calico Pie,
  The little Birds fly
Down to the calico tree,
  Their wings were blue,
  And they sang "Tilly-loo!"
Till away they flew –
    And they never came back to me!
    They never came back!
    They never came back!
    They never came back to me!

Calico Jam,
  The little Fish swam,
Over the syllabub sea,
  He took off his hat,
  To the Sole and the Sprat,
  And the Willeby-wat, –
    But he never came back to me!
    He never came back!
    He never came back!
    He never came back to me!

Calico Ban,
  The little Mice ran,
To be ready in time for tea,
  Flippity flup,
  They drank it all up,
  And danced in the cup, –
    But they never came back to me!
    They never came back!
    They never came back!
    They never came back to me!

Calico Drum,
  The Grasshoppers come,
The Butterfly, Beetle, and Bee,
  Over the ground,
  Around and around,
  With a hop and a bound, –
    But they never came back!
    They never came back!
    They never came back!
    They never came back to me!
                          Edward Lear

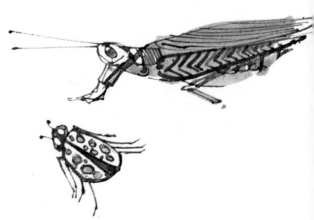

THE GREAT PANJANDRUM

So she went into the garden
to cut a cabbage-leaf
to make an apple-pie;
and at the same time
a great she-bear, coming down the street,
pops its head into the shop.
What! no soap?
  So he died,
and she very imprudently married the Barber:
and there were present
the Picninnies,
    and the Joblillies,
      and the Garyulies,
and the great Panjandrum himself,
with the little round button at top;
and they all fell to playing the game of catch-as-catch-can,
till the gunpowder ran out at the heels of their boots.
                          Samuel Foote

13

There was an old lady of Chertsey,
Who made a remarkable curtsey;
    She twirled round and round,
    Till she sunk underground,
Which distressed all the people of Chertsey.

Edward Lear

THE PESSIMIST

Nothing to do but work,
  Nothing to eat but food,
Nothing to wear but clothes
  To keep one from going nude.

Nothing to breathe but air,
  Quick as a flash 'tis gone;
Nowhere to fall but off,
  Nowhere to stand but on.

Nothing to comb but hair,
  Nowhere to sleep but in bed,
Nothing to weep but tears,
  Nothing to bury but dead.

Nothing to sing but songs,
  Ah, well, alas! alack!
Nowhere to go but out,
  Nowhere to come but back.

Nothing to see but sights,
  Nothing to quench but thirst,
Nothing to have but what we've got;
  Thus thro' life we are cursed.

Nothing to strike but a gait;
  Everything moves that goes.
Nothing at all but common sense
  Can ever withstand these woes.

Ben King

HUMPTY DUMPTY'S POEM

In winter, when the fields are white,
I sing this song for your delight –

In spring, when woods are getting green,
I'll try and tell you what I mean.

In summer, when the days are long,
Perhaps you'll understand the song:

In autumn, when the leaves are brown,
Take pen and ink, and write it down.

I sent a message to the fish:
I told them "This is what I wish."

The little fishes of the sea,
They sent an answer back to me.

The little fishes' answer was
"We cannot do it, Sir, because –"

I sent to them again to say
"It will be better to obey."

The fishes answered with a grin,
"Why, what a temper you are in!"

I told them once, I told them twice:
They would not listen to advice.

I took a kettle large and new,
Fit for the deed I had to do.

My heart went hop, my heart went
                     thump:
I filled the kettle at the pump.

Then someone came to me and said,
"The little fishes are in bed."

I said to him, I said it plain,
"Then you must wake them up again."

I said it very loud and clear;
I went and shouted in his ear.

But he was very stiff and proud;
He said, "You needn't shout so loud!"

And he was very proud and stiff;
He said, "I'd go and wake them, if – "

I took a corkscrew from the shelf:
I went to wake them up myself.

And when I found the door was locked,
I pulled and pushed and kicked and knocked.

And when I found the door was shut,
I tried to turn the handle, but –

Lewis Carroll

THE POBBLE

The Pobble who has no toes
  Had once as many as we;
When they said, "Some day you may lose them all,"
  He replied, "Fish fiddle-de-dee!"
And his Aunt Jobiska made him drink
Lavender water tinged with pink,
For she said, "The World in general knows
There's nothing so good for a Pobble's toes!"

The Pobble who has no toes
  Swam across the Bristol Channel;
But before he set out he wrapped his nose
  In a piece of scarlet flannel,
For his Aunt Jobiska said, "No harm
Can come to his toes if his nose is warm;
And it's perfectly known that a Pobble's toes
Are safe – provided he minds his nose!"

The Pobble swam fast and well,
  And when boats or ships came near him,
He tinkledy-binkledy-winkled a bell,
  So that all the world could hear him,
And all the Sailors and Admirals cried,
When they saw him nearing the further side,
"He has gone to fish for his Aunt Jobiska's
Runcible Cat with crimson whiskers!"

But before he touched the shore,
  The shore of the Bristol Channel,
A sea-green Porpoise carried away
  His wrapper of scarlet flannel,
And when he came to observe his feet,
Formerly garnished with toes so neat,
His face at once became forlorn
On perceiving that all his toes were gone.

And nobody ever knows,
  From that dark day to the present,
Whoso had taken the Pobble's toes,
  In a manner so far from pleasant.
Whether the shrimps or crawfish grey,
Or crafty mermaids stole them away –
Nobody knew; and nobody knows
How the Pobble was robbed of his twice five toes.

The Pobble who has no toes
  Was placed in a friendly Bark,
And they rowed him back, and they carried him up
  To his Aunt Jobiska's Park.
And she made him a feast at his earnest wish
Of eggs and buttercups fried with fish: –
And she said, "It's a fact the whole world knows
That Pobbles are happier without their toes."

Edward Lear

There was an Old Man who said, "How
Shall I flee from this horrible cow?
  I will sit on this stile,
  And continue to smile,
Which may soften the heart of that cow."

Edward Lear

THE KING-FISHER SONG

King Fisher courted Lady Bird –
Sing Beans, sing Bones, sing Butterflies!
  "Find me my match," he said,
  "With such a noble head –
With such a beard, as white as curd –
  With such expressive eyes!"

"Yet pins have heads," said Lady Bird –
Sing Prunes, sing Prawns, sing Primrose-Hill!
  "And, where you stick them in,
  They stay, and thus a pin
Is very much to be preferred
  To one that's never still!"

"Oysters have beards," said Lady Bird –
Sing Flies, sing Frogs, sing Fiddle-strings!
  "I love them, for I know
  They never chatter so:
They would not say one single word –
  Not if you crowned them Kings!"

"Needles have eyes," said Lady Bird –
Sing Cats, sing Corks, sing Cowslip-tea!
  "And they are sharp – just what
  Your Majesty is *not*:
So get you gone – 'tis too absurd
  To come a-courting *me*!"

Lewis Carroll

18

TONY O

Colin Francis

Over the bleak and barren snow
A voice there came a-calling;
"Where are you going to, Tony O!
Where are you going this morning?"

"I am going where there are rivers of wine,
The mountains bread and honey;
There Kings and Queens do mind the swine,
And the poor have all the money."

GET UP AND BAR THE DOOR

It fell about the Martinmas time,
And a gay time it was then,
When our goodwife got puddings to make,
And she's boiled them in the pan.

The wind sae cauld blew south and north,
And blew into the floor;
Quoth our goodman to our goodwife,
"Gae out and bar the door."

"My hand is in my hussyfskap,
Goodman, as ye may see;
An' it shou'dna be barr'd this hundred year,
It's no be barred for me."

They made a paction 'tween them twa,
They made it firm and sure,
That the first word whae'er should speak,
Should rise and bar the door.

Then by there came two gentlemen,
At twelve o'clock at night,
And they could neither see house nor hall,
Nor coal nor candlelight.

"Now whether is this a rich man's house,
Or whether is it a poor?"
But ne'er a word wad ane o' them speak,
For barring of the door.

And first they ate the white puddings,
And then they ate the black.
Tho' muckle thought the goodwife to hersel',
Yet ne'er a word she spake.

Then said the one unto the other,
"Here, man, tak ye my knife;
Do ye tak aff the auld man's beard,
And I'll kiss the goodwife."

"But there's nae water in the house,
And what shall we do than?"
"What ails ye at the pudding-broo,
That boils into the pan?"

O up then started our goodman,
An angry man was he;
"Will ye kiss my wife before my een,
And sca'd me wi' pudding-bree?"

Then up and started our goodwife,
Gied three skips on the floor:
"Goodman, you've spoken the foremost word,
Get up and bar the door."

Anon

IF ALL THE WORLD WERE PAPER

If all the world were paper,
 And all the sea were ink,
And all the trees were bread and cheese,
 What should we do for drink?

If all the world were sand-o,
 Oh, then what should we lack-o?
If, as they say, there were no clay,
 How should we take tobacco?

If all our vessels ran-a,
 If none but had a crack,
If Spanish apes ate all the grapes,
 How should we do for sack?

If friars had no bald pates,
 Nor nuns had no dark cloisters;
If all the seas were beans and peas,
 How should we do for oysters?

If all things were eternal,
 And nothing their end bringing;
If this should be, then how should we
 Here make an end of singing?

Anon

AEIOU

We are very little creatures,
All of different voice and features;
One of us in *glass* is set,
One of us you'll find in *jet*.
T'other you may see in *tin*,
And the fourth a *box* within.
If the fifth you should pursue,
It can never fly from *you*.

Jonathan Swift

I never saw a Purple Cow,
  I never hope to see one;
But I can tell you, anyhow,
  I'd rather see than be one.

Gelett Burgess

A carrion crow sat on an oak,
  Fol de riddle, lol de riddle, hi ding do,
Watching a tailor shape his cloak;
  Sing heigh ho, the carrion crow,
  Fol de riddle, lol de riddle, hi ding do.

Wife, bring me my old bent bow,
  Fol de riddle, lol de riddle, hi ding do,
That I may shoot yon carrion crow;
  Sing heigh ho, the carrion crow,
  Fol de riddle, lol de riddle, hi ding do.

The tailor he shot and missed his mark,
  Fol de riddle, lol de riddle, hi ding do,
And shot his own sow quite through the heart;
  Sing heigh ho, the carrion crow,
  Fol de riddle, lol de riddle, hi ding do.

Wife, bring brandy in a spoon,
  Fol de riddle, lol de riddle, hi ding do,
For our old sow is in a swoon;
  Sing heigh ho, the carrion crow,
  Fol de riddle, lol de riddle, hi ding do.

Anon

My father he died, but I can't tell you how;
He left me six horses to drive in my plough:
    With my wing, wang, waddle oh!
    Strim, stram, straddle oh!
    Blowsy boys, bubble oh!
    Under the broom!

I sold my six horses and I bought me a cow;
I'd fain have made a fortune but I did not know how:
    With my wing, wang, waddle oh!
    Strim, stram, straddle oh!
    Blowsy boys, bubble oh!
    Under the broom!

I sold my cow and I bought me a calf,
I'd fain have made a fortune, but lost the best half:
    With my wing, wang, waddle oh!
    Strim, stram, straddle oh!
    Blowsy boys, bubble oh!
    Under the broom!

I sold my calf, and I bought me a cat,
A pretty thing she was, in my chimney corner sat:
    With my wing, wang, waddle oh!
    Strim, stram, straddle oh!
    Blowsy boys, bubble oh!
    Under the broom!

I sold my cat, and bought me a mouse,
He carried fire in his tail, and burnt down my house:
    With my wing, wang, waddle oh!
    Strim, stram, straddle oh!
    Blowsy boys, bubble oh!
    Under the broom!

Anon

22

NOTTAMUN TOWN

In Nottamun Town not a soul would look up,
Not a soul would look up, not a soul would look down,
Not a soul would look up, not a soul would look down
To tell me the way to Nottamun Town.

I rode a big horse that was called a grey mare,
Grey mane and tail, grey stripes down his back,
Grey mane and tail, grey stripes down his back,
There weren't a hair on him but what was called black.

She stood so still, she threw me to the dirt,
She tore my hide and bruised my shirt;
From stirrup to stirrup I mounted again
And on my ten toes I rode over the plain.

Met the King and the Queen and a company of men
A–walking behind and a–riding before.
A stark naked drummer came walking along
With his hands in his bosom a–beating his drum.

Sat down on a hot and cold frozen stone,
Ten thousand stood round me yet I was alone.
Took my heart in my hand to keep my head warm.
Ten thousand got drowned that never were born.

Anon

There were three jovial Welshmen,
    As I have heard men say,
And they would go a-hunting, boys,
    Upon St. David's Day.
And all the day they hunted,
    But nothing could they find,
Except a ship a-sailing,
    A-sailing with the wind.
        And a-hunting they did go.

One said it surely was a ship,
    The second he said, Nay;
The third declared it was a house
    With the chimney blown away.
Then all the night they hunted,
    And nothing could they find,
Except the moon a-gliding,
    A-gliding with the wind.
        And a-hunting they did go.

One said it surely was the moon,
    The second he said, Nay;
The third declared it was a cheese
    The half o't cut away.
Then all next day they hunted,
    And nothing could they find,
Except a hedgehog in a bush,
    And that they left behind.
        And a-hunting they did go.

One said it was a hedgehog,
    The second he said, Nay;
The third, it was a pincushion,
    The pins stuck in wrong way.
Then all next night they hunted,
    And nothing could they find,
Except a hare in a turnip field,
    And that they left behind.
        And a-hunting they did go.

One said it surely was a hare,
    The second he said, Nay;
The third, he said it was a calf,
    And the cow had run away.
Then all next day they hunted,
    And nothing could they find,
But one owl in a holly-tree,
    And that they left behind.
        And a-hunting they did go.

One said it surely was an owl,
    The second he said, Nay;
The third said 'twas an aged man
    Whose beard was growing grey.
Then all three jovial Welshmen
    Came riding home at last,
"For three days we have nothing killed,
    And never broke our fast!"
        And a-hunting they did go.

Anon

Sir Eglamour, that worthy knight,
He took his sword and went to fight:
And as he rode both hill and dale,
Armed upon his shirt of mail,
A dragon came out of his den,
Had slain, God knows how many men!

When he espied Sir Eglamour,
Oh, if you had but heard him roar,
And seen how all the trees did shake,
The knights did tremble, horse did quake,
The birds betake them all to peeping –
It would have made you fall a-weeping!

But now it is in vain to fear,
Being come unto, "fight dog! fight bear!"
To it they go and fiercely fight
A live-long day from morn till night.
The dragon had a plaguy hide,
And could the sharpest steel abide.

No sword will enter him with cuts,
Which vexed the knight unto the guts;
But, as in choler he did burn,
He watched the dragon a good turn;
And, as a-yawning he did fall,
He thrust his sword in, hilts and all.

There, like a coward, he to fly
Unto his den that was hard by;
And there he lay all night and roared.
The knight was sorry for his sword,
But, riding thence, said, "I forsake it,
He that will fetch it, let him take it!"

Anon

I saw a peacock with a fiery tail
I saw a blazing comet drop down hail
I saw a cloud wrapped with ivy round
I saw an oak creep upon the ground
I saw a pismire swallow up a whale
I saw the sea brimful of ale
I saw a Venice glass full fifteen feet deep
I saw a well full of men's tears that weep
I saw red eyes all of a flaming fire
I saw a house bigger than the moon and higher
I saw the sun at twelve o'clock at night
I saw the man that saw this wondrous sight.

Anon

CHILDREN, YOU ARE VERY LITTLE

My mother said I never should
Play with the gipsies in the wood;
If I did, she would say,
Naughty girl to disobey.
Your hair shan't curl
And your shoes shan't shine,
You gipsy girl,
You shan't be mine.

And my father said that if I did
He'd rap my head with the tea-pot lid.
The wood was dark; the grass was green;
In came Sally with a tambourine.
I went to the sea – no ship to get across;
I paid ten shillings for a blind white horse;
I up on his back and was off in a crack,
Sally tell my mother I shall never come back.

Anon

28

Don't-care didn't care;
  Don't-care was wild.
Don't-care stole plum and pear
  Like any beggar's child.

Don't-care was made to care,
  Don't-care was hung;
Don't-care was put in the pot
  And boiled till he was done.

Anon

JEMIMA

There was a little girl, and she wore a little curl
  Right down the middle of her forehead.
When she was good, she was very, very good,
  But when she was bad, she was horrid!

One day she went upstairs, while her parents, unawares,
  In the kitchen down below were occupied with meals,
And she stood upon her head, on her little truckle bed,
  And she then began hurraying with her heels.

Her mother heard the noise, and thought it was the boys
  A-playing at a combat in the attic,
But when she climbed the stair and saw Jemima there,
  She took and she did whip her most emphatic.

Anon

SPEAK ROUGHLY TO YOUR LITTLE BOY

Speak roughly to your little boy,
  And beat him when he sneezes;
He only does it to annoy,
  Because he knows it teases.
    Wow! Wow! Wow!

I speak severely to my boy,
  I beat him when he sneezes;
For he can thoroughly enjoy
  The pepper when he pleases!
    Wow! Wow! Wow!

Lewis Carroll

MATILDA
Who told Lies, and was Burned to Death

Matilda told such Dreadful Lies,
It made one Gasp and Stretch one's Eyes;
Her Aunt, who, from her Earliest Youth,
Had kept a Strict Regard for Truth,
Attempted to Believe Matilda:
The effort very nearly killed her,
And would have done so, had not She
Discovered this Infirmity.
For once, towards the Close of Day,
Matilda, growing tired of play,
And finding she was left alone,
Went tiptoe to the Telephone
And summoned the Immediate Aid
Of London's Noble Fire-Brigade.
Within an hour the Gallant Band
Were pouring in on every hand,
From Putney, Hackney Downs and Bow,
With Courage high and Hearts a-glow
They galloped, roaring through the Town,
"Matilda's House is Burning Down!"
Inspired by British Cheers and Loud
Proceeding from the Frenzied Crowd,
They ran their ladders through a score
Of windows on the Ball Room Floor;
And took Peculiar Pains to Souse
The Pictures up and down the House,
Until Matilda's Aunt succeeded
In showing them they were not needed,
And even then she had to pay
To get the Men to go away!

It happened that a few Weeks later
Her Aunt was off to the Theatre
To see that Interesting Play
The Second Mrs. Tanqueray.
She had refused to take her Niece
To hear this Entertaining Piece:
A Deprivation Just and Wise
To Punish her for Telling Lies.
That Night a Fire *did* break out –
You should have heard Matilda Shout!
You should have heard her Scream and Bawl,
And throw the window up and call
To People passing in the Street –
(The rapidly increasing Heat
Encouraging her to obtain
Their confidence) – but all in vain!
For every time she shouted "Fire!"
They only answered "Little Liar!"
And therefore when her Aunt returned,
Matilda, and the House, were Burned.

Hilaire Belloc

GOOD AND BAD CHILDREN

Children, you are very little,
And your bones are very brittle;
If you would grow great and stately,
You must try to walk sedately.

You must still be bright and quiet,
And content with simple diet;
And remain, through all bewild'ring,
Innocent and honest children.

Happy hearts and happy faces,
Happy play in grassy places –
That was how, in ancient ages,
Children grew to kings and sages.

But the unkind and the unruly,
And the sort who eat unduly,
They must never hope for glory –
Theirs is quite a different story!

Cruel children, crying babies,
All grow up as geese and gabies,
Hated, as their age increases,
By their nephews and their nieces.

R. L. Stevenson

If I should ever by chance grow rich
I'll buy Codham, Cockridden, and Childerditch,
Roses, Pyrgo, and Lapwater,
And let them all to my elder daughter.
The rent I shall ask of her will be only
Each year's first violets, white and lonely,
The first year's primroses and orchises –
She must find them before I do, that is.
But if she finds a blossom on furze
Without rent they shall all for ever be hers,
Whenever I am sufficiently rich:
Codham, Cockridden, and Childerditch,
Roses, Pyrgo and Lapwater –
I shall give them all to my elder daughter.

Edward Thomas

WARNING TO CHILDREN

Children, if you dare to think
Of the greatness, rareness, muchness,
Fewness of this precious only
Endless world in which you say
You live, you think of things like this:
Blocks of slate enclosing dappled
Red and green, enclosing tawny
Yellow nets, enclosing white
And black acres of dominoes,
Where a neat brown paper parcel
Tempts you to untie the string.
In the parcel a small island,
On the island a large tree,
On the tree a husky fruit.
Strip the husk and cut the rind off:
In the centre you will see
Blocks of slate enclosed by dappled
Red and green, enclosed by tawny
Yellow nets, enclosed by white

And black acres of dominoes,
Where the same brown paper parcel –
Children, leave the string untied!
For who dares undo the parcel
Finds himself at once inside it,
On the island, in the fruit,
Blocks of slate about his head,
Finds himself enclosed by dappled
Green and red, enclosed by yellow
Tawny nets, enclosed by black
And white acres of dominoes,
But the same brown paper parcel
Still untied upon his knee.
And, if he then should dare to think
Of the fewness, muchness, rareness,
Greatness of this endless only
Precious world in which he says
He lives – he then unties the string.

Robert Graves

THERE I MET A PRETTY MISS

I WILL GIVE MY LOVE
AN APPLE

I will give my love an apple without e'er a core,
I will give my love a house without e'er a door,
I will give my love a palace wherein she may be,
And she may unlock it without any key.

My head is the apple without e'er a core,
My mind is the house without e'er a door,
My heart is the palace wherein she may be,
And she may unlock it without any key.

Anon

As I was going up Pippin Hill,
  Pippin Hill was dirty,
There I met a pretty miss,
  And she dropped me a curtsey.

"Little miss, pretty miss,
  Blessings light upon you!
If I had half a crown a day,
  I'd spend it all upon you."

Anon

Soldier, soldier, won't you marry me?
  It's O the fife and the drum!
How can I marry such a pretty girl as you
  When I've got no hat to put on!

Off to the tailor's she did go
  As fast as she could run,
Brought him back the finest that was there:
  Now, soldier, put it on!

Soldier, soldier, won't you marry me?
  It's O the fife and the drum!
How can I marry such a pretty girl as you
  When I've got no coat to put on!

Back to the tailor's she did go
  As fast as she could run,
Brought him back the finest that was there:
  Now, soldier, put it on!

Soldier, soldier, won't you marry me?
  It's O the fife and the drum!
How can I marry such a pretty girl as you
  When I've got no shoes to put on!

Off to the shoe-shop she did go
  As fast as she could run,
Brought him back the finest that were there:
  Now, soldier, put them on!

Soldier, soldier, won't you marry me?
  It's O the fife and the drum!
How can I marry such a pretty girl as you
  When I've a wife and babies at home!

Anon

THREE KNIGHTS FROM SPAIN

We are three Brethren come from Spain,
   All in French garlands;
We are come to court your daughter, Jane,
   And adieu to you, my darlings.

My daughter Jane! – she is too young,
   All in French garlands,
She cannot bide your flattering tongue,
   And adieu to you, my darlings.

Be she young, or be she old,
   All in French garlands,
'Tis for a bride she must be sold,
   And adieu to you, my darlings.

A bride, a bride, she shall not be,
   All in French garlands,
Till she go through this world with me,
   And adieu to you, my darlings.

Then shall you keep your daughter, Jane,
   All in French garlands,
Come once, we come not here again,
   And adieu to you, my darlings.

Turn back, turn back, you Spanish Knights,
  All in French garlands;
Scour, scour your spurs, till they be bright,
  And adieu to you, my darlings.

Sharp shine our spurs all richly wrought,
  All in French garlands,
In towns afar our spurs were bought,
  And adieu to you, my darlings.

Smell my lilies, smell my roses,
  All in French garlands;
Which of my maidens do you choose?
  And adieu to you, my darlings.

Not she, not she. Thy youngest, Jane!
  All in French garlands;
We ride – and ride not back again,
  And adieu to you, my darlings.

In every pocket a thousand pound,
  All in French garlands;
On every finger a gay gold ring,
  And adieu to you, my darlings,
    And adieu to you, my darlings.

Anon

He was a rat, and she was a rat,
  And down in one hole they did dwell,
And both were as black as a witch's cat,
  And they loved one another well.

He had a tail, and she had a tail,
  Both long and curling and fine;
And each said, "Yours is the finest tail
  In the world, excepting mine."

He smelt the cheese, and she smelt the cheese,
  And they both pronounced it good;
And both remarked it would greatly add
  To the charms of their daily food.

So he ventured out, and she ventured out,
  And I saw them go with pain,
But what befell them I never can tell,
  For they never came back again.

Anon

GREEN BROOM

There was an old man lived out in the wood,
His trade was a-cutting of Broom, green Broom;
He had but one son without thrift, without good,
Who lay in his bed till 'twas noon, bright noon.

The old man awoke one morning and spoke,
He swore he would fire the room, that room,
If his John would not rise and open his eyes,
And away to the wood to cut Broom, green Broom;

So Johnny arose, and he slipped on his clothes,
And away to the wood to cut Broom, green Broom;
He sharpened his knives, for once he contrives
To cut a great bundle of Broom, green Broom.

When Johnny passed under a lady's fine house,
Passed under a lady's fine room, fine room,
She called to her maid, "Go fetch me," she said,
"Go fetch me the boy that sells Broom, green Broom."

When Johnny came in to the lady's fine house,
And stood in the lady's fine room, fine room;
"Young Johnny," she said, "will you give up your trade,
And marry a lady in bloom, full bloom?"

Johnny gave his consent, and to church they both went,
And he wedded the lady in bloom, full bloom.
At market and fair, all folks do declare,
There is none like the boy that sold Broom, green Broom.

Anon

A knight came riding from the East,
 Jennifer, gentle and rosemarie,
Who had been wooing at many a place,
 As the dove flies over the mulberry tree.

He came and knocked at the lady's gate,
One evening when it was growing late.

The eldest sister let him in,
And pinned the door with a silver pin.

The second sister, she made his bed
And laid soft pillows under his head.

The youngest sister was bold and bright
And she would wed with this unco'
                              knight.

"If you will answer me questions three,
This very day will I marry thee.

"O what is louder nor a horn?
And what is sharper nor a thorn?

"What is heavier nor the lead?
And what is better nor the bread?

"O what is higher nor the tree?
And what is deeper nor the sea?"

"O, shame is louder nor a horn,
And hunger is sharper nor a thorn.

"And sin is heavier nor the lead,
And the blessing's better nor the bread.

"O, Heaven is higher nor the tree,
And love is deeper nor the sea."

"O, you have answered my questions three,
    Jennifer, gentle and rosemarie,
And so, fair maid, I'll marry with thee,
    As the dove flies over the mulberry tree."

                                        Anon

FLOWERS IN THE VALLEY

O there was a woman, and she was a widow,
Fair are the flowers in the valley.
With a daughter as fair as a fresh sunny meadow,
The Red, the Green, and the Yellow.
The Harp, the Lute, the Pipe, the Flute, the Cymbal,
Sweet goes the treble Violin.
The maid so rare and the flowers so fair
Together they grew in the valley.

There came a Knight all clothed in red,
Fair are the flowers in the valley.
"I would thou wert my bride," he said,
The Red, the Green, and the Yellow.
The Harp, the Lute, the Pipe, the Flute, the Cymbal,
Sweet goes the treble Violin.
"I would," she sighed, "ne'er wins a bride!"
Fair are the flowers in the valley.

There came a Knight all clothed in green,
Fair are the flowers in the valley.
"This maid so sweet might be my queen,"
The Red, the Green, and the Yellow.
The Harp, the Lute, the Pipe, the Flute, the Cymbal,
Sweet goes the treble Violin.
"Might be," sighed she, "will ne'er win me!"
Fair are the flowers in the valley.

There came a Knight, in yellow was he,
Fair are the flowers in the valley.
"My bride, my queen, thou must with me!"
The Red, the Green, and the Yellow.
The Harp, the Lute, the Pipe, the Flute, the Cymbal,
Sweet goes the treble Violin.
With blushes red, "I come," she said;
"Farewell to the flowers in the valley."

Anon

A BIRTHDAY

My heart is like a singing bird
    Whose nest is in a watered shoot:
My heart is like an apple-tree
    Whose boughs are bent with thickset fruit;
My heart is like a rainbow shell
    That paddles in a halcyon sea;
My heart is gladder than all these
    Because my love is come to me.

Raise me a dais of silk and down;
    Hang it with vair and purple dyes;
Carve it in doves and pomegranates,
    And peacocks with a hundred eyes;
Work it in gold and silver grapes,
    In leaves and silver fleurs-de-lys;
Because the birthday of my life
    Is come, my love is come to me.

Christina Rossetti

Pack, clouds, away! and welcome, day!
  With night we banish sorrow:
Sweet air, blow soft! mount, lark, aloft!
  To give my Love good-morrow;
Wings from the wind, to please her mind,
  Notes from the lark I'll borrow.
Bird, prune thy wing! nightingale, sing!
  To give my Love good-morrow.
  To give my Love good-morrow
  Notes from them all I'll borrow.

Wake from thy nest, robin redbreast!
  Sing, birds, in every furrow!
And from each bill let music shrill
  Give my fair Love good-morrow.
Blackbird and thrush, in every bush –
  Stare, linnet, and cock-sparrow,
You pretty elves, among yourselves
  Sing my fair Love good-morrow!
  To give my Love good-morrow
  Sing, birds, in every furrow.

                    Thomas Heywood

THE WORLD OF WATERS IS OUR HOME

THE DEATH OF ADMIRAL BENBOW

Come all you sailors bold,
  Lend an ear,
Come all you sailors bold,
  Lend an ear:
'Tis of our Admiral's fame,
Brave Benbow called by name,
How he fought on the main
  You shall hear.

Brave Benbow he set sail
  For to fight,
Brave Benbow he set sail
  For to fight:
Brave Benbow he set sail,
With a fine and pleasant gale,
But his captains they turned tail
  In a fight.

Says Kirkby unto Wade,
  "I will run,"
Says Kirkby unto Wade,
  "I will run:
I value not disgrace,
Nor the losing of my place,
My foes I will not face
  With a gun."

'Twas the *Ruby* and *Noah's Ark*,
  Fought the French,
'Twas the *Ruby* and *Noah's Ark*,
  Fought the French:
And there was ten in all,
Poor souls they fought them all,
They recked them not at all
  Nor their noise.

It was our Admiral's lot,
  With a chain-shot,
It was our Admiral's lot,
  With a chain-shot:
Our Admiral lost his legs,
And to his men he begs
"Fight on, my boys," he says,
  "'Tis my lot."

While the surgeon dressed his wounds,
  Thus he said,
While the surgeon dressed his wounds,
  Thus he said:
"Let my cradle now in haste
On the quarter-deck be placed,
That the Frenchmen I may face,
  Till I'm dead."

And there bold Benbow lay,
  Crying out,
And there bold Benbow lay,
  Crying out:
"O let us tack once more,
We'll drive them to the shore,
As our fathers did before
  Long ago."

Anon

A wet sheet and a flowing sea,
  A wind that follows fast,
And fills the white and rustling sail,
  And bends the gallant mast;
And bends the gallant mast, my boys,
  While, like the eagle free,
Away the good ship flies, and leaves
  Old England on the lee.

O for a soft and gentle wind!
  I heard a fair one cry;
But give to me the snoring breeze,
  And white waves heaving high;
And the white waves heaving high, my boys,
  The good ship tight and free –
The world of waters is our home,
  And merry men are we.

There's tempest in yon horned moon,
  And lightning in yon cloud;
And hark the music, mariners!
  The wind is piping loud,
The wind is piping loud, my boys,
  The lightning flashing free –
While the hollow oak our palace is,
  Our heritage the sea.

Allan Cunningham

46

SIR PATRICK SPENS

I. *The Sailing*

The king sits in Dunfermline town,
  Drinking the blude-red wine;
"O whar will I get a skeely skipper
  To sail this new ship o' mine?"

Up and spak an eldern knight,
  Sat at the king's right knee:
"Sir Patrick Spens is the best sailor
  That ever sail'd the sea."

Our king has written a braid letter,
  And seal'd it wi' his hand,
And sent it to Sir Patrick Spens,
  Was walking on the strand.

"To Noroway, to Noroway,
  To Noroway o'er the faem;
The king's daughter o' Noroway,
  'Tis thou maun bring her hame."

The first word that Sir Patrick read
  A loud laugh laughed he;
The neist word that Sir Patrick read,
  The tear blinded his e'e.

"O wha is this has done this deed
  And tauld the king o' me,
To send us out, at this time o' year,
  To sail upon the sea?

"Be it wind, be it weet, be it hail, be it sleet,
  Our ship must sail the faem;
The king's daughter o' Noroway,
  'Tis we maun fetch her hame."

They hoysed their sails on Monenday morn
  Wi' a' the speed they may;
They ha'e landed in Noroway
  Upon a Wodensday.

II. *The Return*

"Mak ready, mak ready, my merry men a'!
    Our gude ship sails the morn." –
"Now ever alack, my master dear,
    I fear a deadly storm!

"I saw the new moon late yestreen
    Wi' the auld moon in her arm;
And if we gang to sea, master,
    I fear we'll come to harm!"

They hadna' sailed a league, a league,
    A league but barely three,
When the lift grew dark, and the wind blew loud,
    And gurly grew the sea.

The anchors brak, and the topmast lap
    It was sic a deadly storm;
And the waves cam owre the broken ship
    Till a' her sides were torn.

"O whar will I get a gude sailor
    To tak my helm in hand,
Till I get up to the tall topmast
    To see if I can spy land?" –

"Oh here am I, a sailor gude,
    To tak the helm in hand,
Till you go up to the tall topmast,
But I fear you'll ne'er spy land."

He hadna gane a step, a step,
    A step but barely ane,
When a bolt flew out of our goodly ship,
    And the saut sea it came in.

"Gae fetch a web o' the silken claith,
    Another o' the twine,
And wap them into our ship's side,
    And let na' the sea come in."

They fetched a web o' the silken claith,
    Another o' the twine,
And they wrapped them round that gude ship's side,
    But still the sea cam in.

O laith, laith were our gude Scots lords
    To wet their cork-heel'd shoon;
But lang or a' the play was play'd
    They wet their hats aboon.

And mony was the feather bed
    That flatter'd on the faem;
And mony was the gude laird's son
    That never mair cam hame.

O lang, lang may the ladies sit,
    Wi' their fans into their hand,
Before they see Sir Patrick Spens
    Come sailing to the strand!

And lang, lang may the maidens sit
    Wi' their gowd kames in their hair,
A' waiting for their ain dear loves!
    For them they'll see nae mair.

Half-owre, half-owre to Aberdour,
    'Tis fifty fathoms deep;
And there lies gude Sir Patrick Spens
    Wi' the Scots lords at his feet!

Anon

Skeely, skilful; *braid,* plain; *faem*, foam; *maun*, must; *neist*, next; *hoysed*, hoisted; *lift*, sky; *gurly*, stormy; *lap*, sprang; *saut*, salt; *claith*, cloth; *wap*, wrap; *laith*, unwilling; *kames*, combs.

THE COASTS OF HIGH BARBARY

Look ahead, look astern, look the weather and the lee.
Blow high! blow low! and so sail-ed we.
I see a wreck to windward and a lofty ship to lee,
A-sailing down all on the coasts of High Barbary.

O are you a pirate or man-o'-war, cried we?
Blow high! blow low! and so sail-ed we.
O no! I'm not a pirate, but a man-o'-war, cried he,
A-sailing down all on the coasts of High Barbary.

Then back up your topsails and heave your vessel to,
Blow high! blow low! and so sail-ed we.
For we have got some letters to be carried home by you,
A-sailing down all on the coasts of High Barbary.

We'll back up our topsails and heave our vessel to;
Blow high! blow low! and so sail-ed we,
But only in some harbour and along the side of you,
A-sailing down all on the coasts of High Barbary.

For broadside, for broadside, they fought all on the main;
Blow high! blow low! and so sail-ed we,
Until at last the frigate shot the pirate's mast away,
A-sailing down all on the coasts of High Barbary.

For quarters! for quarters! the saucy pirate cried.
Blow high! blow low! and so sail-ed we.
The quarters that we showed them was to sink them in the tide,
A-sailing down all on the coasts of High Barbary.

With cutlass and gun O we fought for hours three;
Blow high! blow low! and so sail-ed we.
The ship it was their coffin, and their grave it was the sea,
A-sailing down all on the coasts of High Barbary.

But O! it was a cruel sight, and griev-ed us full sore,
Blow high! blow low! and so sail-ed we.
To see them all a-drowning as they tried to swim to shore
A-sailing down all on the coasts of High Barbary.

Anon

POSTED AS MISSING

Under all her topsails she trembled like a stag,
The wind made a ripple in her bonny red flag;
They cheered her from the shore and they cheered her from the pier,
And under all her topsails she trembled like a deer.

So she passed swaying, where the green seas run,
Her wind-steadied topsails were stately in the sun;
There was glitter on the water from her red port light,
So she passed swaying, till she was out of sight.

Long and long ago it was, a weary time it is,
The bones of her sailor-men are coral plants by this;
Coral plants, and shark-weed, and a mermaid's comb,
And if the fishers net them they never bring them home.

It's rough on sailors' women. They have to mangle hard
And stitch at dungarees till their finger-ends are scarred,
Thinking of the sailor-men who sang among the crows,
Hoisting of her topsails when she sailed so proud.

John Masefield

Break, break, break,
   On thy cold grey stones, O Sea!
And I would that my tongue could utter
   The thoughts that arise in me.

O well for the fisherman's boy,
   That he shouts with his sister at play!
O well for the sailor lad,
   That he sings in his boat on the bay!

And the stately ships go on
   To their haven under the hill;
But O for the touch of a vanish'd hand,
   And the sound of a voice that is still!

Break, break, break,
   At the foot of thy crags, O Sea!
But the tender grace of a day that is dead
   Will never come back to me.

Alfred, Lord Tennyson

ARIEL'S SONG

Full fathom five thy father lies;
    Of his bones are coral made;
Those are pearls that were his eyes:
    Nothing of him that doth fade,
But doth suffer a sea-change
Into something rich and strange:
Sea-nymphs hourly ring his knell.
    Ding-dong!
Hark! now I hear them,
– Ding-dong, bell!

William Shakespeare

A SMUGGLERS' SONG

If you wake at midnight and hear a horse's feet,
Don't go drawing back the blind, or looking in the street,
Them that asks no questions isn't told a lie.
Watch the wall, my darling, while the Gentlemen go by!
                Five and twenty ponies,
                Trotting through the dark –
                Brandy for the Parson,
                'Baccy for the Clerk;
                Laces for a lady; letters for a spy,
And watch the wall, my darling, while the Gentlemen go by!

Running round the woodlump if you chance to find
Little barrels, roped and tarred, all full of brandy-wine;
Don't you shout to come and look, nor take 'em for your play;
Put the brushwood back again, – and they'll be gone next day!

If you see the stableyard setting open wide;
If you see a tired horse lying down inside;
If your mother mends a coat cut about and tore;
If the lining's wet and warm – don't you ask no more!

If you meet King George's men, dressed in blue and red,
You be careful what you say, and mindful what is said.
If they call you "pretty maid", and chuck you 'neath the chin,
Don't you tell where no one is, nor yet where no one's been!

Knocks and footsteps round the house – whistles after dark –
You've no call for running out till the housedogs bark.
Trusty's here and Pincher's here, and see how dumb they lie –
They don't fret to follow when the Gentlemen go by!

If you do as you've been told, likely there's a chance,
You'll be give a dainty doll, all the way from France,
With a cap of Valenciennes, and a velvet hood –
A present from the Gentlemen, along o' being good!
        Five and twenty ponies,
        Trotting through the dark –
        Brandy for the Parson,
        'Baccy for the Clerk.
Them that asks no questions isn't told a lie –
Watch the wall, my darling, while the Gentlemen go by!
                        Rudyard Kipling

THE JUMBLIES

I

They went to sea in a Sieve, they did,
  In a Sieve they went to sea:
In spite of all their friends could say,
On a winter's morn, on a stormy day,
  In a Sieve they went to sea!
And when the Sieve turned round and round,
And every one cried, "You'll all be drowned!"
They called aloud, "Our Sieve ain't big,
But we don't care a button! we don't care a fig!
  In a Sieve we'll go to sea!"
    Far and few, far and few,
      Are the lands where the Jumblies live;
    Their heads are green, and their hands are blue,
      And they went to sea in a Sieve.

II

They sailed away in a Sieve, they did,
  In a Sieve they sailed so fast,
With only a beautiful pea-green veil
Tied with a riband by way of a sail,
  To a small tobacco-pipe mast;
And everyone said, who saw them go,
"O won't they be soon upset, you know!
For the sky is dark, and the voyage is long,
And happen what may, it's extremely wrong
  In a Sieve to sail so fast!"
    Far and few, far and few,
      Are the lands where the Jumblies live;
    Their heads are green, and their hands are blue,
      And they went to sea in a Sieve.

III

The water it soon came in, it did,
  The water it soon came in;
So to keep them dry, they wrapped their feet
In a pinky paper all folded neat,
  And they fastened it down with a pin.
And they passed the night in a crockery-jar,
And each of them said, "How wise we are!
Though the sky be dark, and the voyage be long,
Yet we never can think we were rash or wrong,
  While round in our Sieve we spin!"
    Far and few, far and few,
      Are the lands where the Jumblies live;
      Their heads are green, and their hands are blue,
      And they went to sea in a Sieve.

IV

And all night long they sailed away;
  And when the sun went down,
They whistled and warbled a moony song
To the echoing sound of a coppery gong,
  In the shade of the mountains brown.
"O Timballo! How happy we are,
When we live in a Sieve and a crockery-jar,
And all night long in the moonlight pale,
We sail away with a pea-green sail,
  In the shade of the mountains brown!"
    Far and few, far and few,
      Are the lands where the Jumblies live;
      Their heads are green, and their hands are blue,
      And they went to sea in a Sieve.

V

They sailed to the Western Sea, they did,
   To a land all covered with trees,
And they bought an Owl, and a useful Cart,
And a pound of Rice, and a Cranberry Tart,
   And a hive of silvery Bees.
And they bought a Pig, and some green Jack-daws,
And a lovely Monkey with lollipop paws,
And forty bottles of Ring-Bo-Ree,
   And no end of Stilton Cheese.
     Far and few, far and few,
      Are the lands where the Jumblies live;
     Their heads are green and their hands are blue,
      And they went to sea in a Sieve.

VI

And in twenty years they all came back,
   In twenty years or more,
And every one said, "How tall they've grown!
For they've been to the Lakes, and the Torrible Zone,
   And the hills of the Chankly Bore;"
And they drank their health, and gave them a feast
Of dumplings made of beautiful yeast;
And every one said, "If we only live,
We too will go to sea in a Sieve, –
   To the hills of the Chankly Bore!"
     Far and few, far and few,
      Are the lands where the Jumblies live;
     Their heads are green, and their hands are blue,
      And they went to sea in a Sieve.

Edward Lear

THE GOLDEN VANITY

A ship I have got in the North Country
And she goes by the name of the *Golden Vanity*.
O I fear she'll be taken by a Spanish Ga-la-lee,
   As she sails by the Lowlands low.

To the captain then upspake the little cabin-boy,
He said, "What is my fee, if the galley I destroy?
The Spanish Ga-la-lee if no more it shall annoy,
   As you sail by the Lowlands low."

"Of silver and of gold I will give to you a store;
And my pretty little daughter that dwelleth on the shore.
Of treasure and of fee as well, I'll give to thee galore,
   As we sail by the Lowlands low."

Then they row'd him up tight in a black bull's skin,
And he held all in his hand an augur sharp and thin,
And he swam until he came to the Spanish Gal-a-lin,
   As she lay by the Lowlands low.

He bored with his augur, he bored once and twice,
And some were playing cards, and some were playing dice,
When the water flowed in it dazzled their eyes,
   And she sank by the Lowlands low.

So the cabin-boy did swim all to the larboard side,
Saying "Captain! take me in, I am drifting with the tide!"
"I will shoot you! I will kill you!" the cruel captain cried,
   "You may sink by the Lowlands low."

Then the cabin-boy did swim all to the starboard side,
Saying, "Messmates, take me in, I am drifting with the tide!"
Then they laid him on the deck, and he closed his eyes and died,
   As they sailed by the Lowlands low.

They sew'd his body tight in an old cow's hide,
And they cast the gallant cabin-boy out over the ship's side,
And left him without more ado to drift with the tide,
   And to sink by the Lowlands low.

Anon

THE SOUND OF THE WIND

The wind has such a rainy sound
   Moaning through the town,
The sea has such a windy sound, –
   Will the ships go down?

The apples in the orchard
   Tumble from their tree. –
Oh will the ships go down, go down,
   In the windy sea?

Christina Rossetti

THE FORSAKEN MERMAN

Come, dear children, let us away;
Down and away below.
Now my brothers call from the bay;
Now the great winds shorewards blow;
Now the salt tides seawards flow;
Now the wild white horses play,
Champ and chafe and toss in the spray.
Children dear, let us away.
This way, this way.

Call her once before you go.
Call once yet.
In a voice that she will know:
"Margaret! Margaret!"
Children's voices should be dear
(Call once more) to a mother's ear:
Children's voices, wild with pain.
Surely she will come again.
Call her once and come away.
This way, this way.
"Mother dear, we cannot stay."
The wild white horses foam and fret.
Margaret! Margaret!

Come, dear children, come away down.
Call no more.
One last look at the white-wall'd town,
And the little grey church on the windy shore.
Then come down.
She will not come though you call all day.
Come away, come away.

Children dear, was it yesterday
We heard the sweet bells over the bay?
In the caverns where we lay,
Through the surf and through the swell,
The far-off sound of a silver bell?
Sand-strewn caverns, cool and deep,
Where the winds are all asleep;
Where the spent lights quiver and gleam;
Where the salt weed sways in the stream;
Where the sea-beasts rang'd all round
Feed in the ooze of their pasture-ground;
Where the sea-snakes coil and twine,
Dry their mail and bask in the brine;
Where great whales come sailing by,
Sail and sail, with unshut eye,
Round the world for ever and aye?
When did music come this way?
Children dear, was it yesterday?

Children dear, was it yesterday
(Call yet once) that she went away?
Once she sate with you and me,
On a red gold throne in the heart of the sea,
And the youngest sate on her knee.
She comb'd its bright hair, and she tended it well,
When down swung the sound of the far-off bell.
She sigh'd, she look'd up through the clear green sea.
She said: "I must go, for my kinsfolk pray
In the little grey church on the shore to-day.
'Twill be Easter-time in the world – ah me!
And I lose my poor soul, Merman, here with thee."
I said: "Go up, dear heart, through the waves;
Say thy prayer, and come back to the kind sea-caves."
She smil'd, she went up through the surf in the bay.
Children dear, was it yesterday?

Children dear, were we long alone?
"The sea grows stormy, the little ones moan.
Long prayers," I said, "in the world they say.
Come," I said, and we rose through the surf in the bay.
We went up the beach, by the sandy down
Where the sea-stocks bloom, to the white-wall'd town.

Through the narrow pav'd streets, where all was still,
To the little grey church on the windy hill.
From the church came a murmur of folk at their prayers,
But we stood without in the cold blowing airs.
We climb'd on the graves, on the stones, worn with rains,
And we gaz'd up the aisle through the small leaded panes.
She sate by the pillar; we saw her clear:
"Margaret, hist! come quick, we are here.
Dear heart," I said, "we are long alone.
The sea grows stormy, the little ones moan."
But, ah, she gave me never a look,
For her eyes were seal'd to the holy book.
Loud prays the priest; shut stands the door.
Come away, children, call no more.
Come away, come down, call no more.

Down, down, down.
Down to the depths of the sea.
She sits at her wheel in the humming town,
Singing most joyfully.
Hark, what she sings; "O joy, O joy,
For the humming street, and the child with its toy.
For the priest, and the bell, and the holy well.
For the wheel where I spun,
And the blessed light of the sun."
And so she sings her fill,
Singing most joyfully,
Till the shuttle falls from her hand,
And the whizzing wheel stands still.
She steals to the window, and looks at the sand;
And over the sand at the sea;
And her eyes are set in a stare;
And anon there breaks a sigh,
And anon there drops a tear,
From a sorrow-clouded eye,
And a heart sorrow-laden,
A long, long sigh,
For the cold strange eyes of a little Mermaiden,
And the gleam of her golden hair.

Come away, away, children.
Come children, come down.
The hoarse wind blows colder;
Lights shine in the town.
She will start from her slumber
When gusts shake the door;
She will hear the winds howling,
Will hear the waves roar.
We shall see, while above us
The waves roar and whirl,
A ceiling of amber,
A pavement of pearl.
Singing, "Here came a mortal,
But faithless was she.
And alone dwell for ever
The kings of the sea."

But, children, at midnight,
When soft the winds blow;
When clear falls the moonlight;
When spring-tides are low:
When sweet airs come seaward
From heaths starr'd with broom;
And high rocks throw mildly
On the blanch'd sands a gloom;
Up the still, glistening beaches,
Up the creeks we will hie;
Over banks of bright seaweed
The ebb-tide leaves dry.
We will gaze, from the sand-hills,
At the white, sleeping town;
At the church on the hill-side –
And then come back down.
Singing, "There dwells a lov'd one,
But cruel is she.
She left lonely for ever
The kings of the sea."

Matthew Arnold

WHAT BIRD SO SINGS?

THE ROBIN AND THE WREN

The robin and the redbreast,
    The robin and the wren,
If you take them out of their nest,
    Ye'll ne'er thrive again.

The robin and the redbreast,
    The martin and the swallow;
If you touch one of their eggs,
    Ill luck is sure to follow.

Anon

A pye sat on a pear-tree,
A pye sat on a pear-tree,
A pye sat on a pear-tree,
    Heigh-Ho! Heigh-Ho! Heigh-Ho!

Once so merrily hopped she,
Twice so merrily hopped she,
Thrice so merrily hopped she,
    Heigh-Ho! Heigh-Ho! Heigh-Ho!

Anon

SONG

I had a dove and the sweet dove died;
    And I have thought it died of grieving:
O, what could it grieve for? its feet were tied
    With a silken thread of my own hand's weaving;
Sweet little red feet! why should you die –
Why should you leave me, sweet bird! why?
    You liv'd alone in the forest-tree,
Why, pretty thing! would you not live with me?
I kiss'd you oft and gave you white peas;
Why not live sweetly, as in the green trees?

John Keats

LITTLE TROTTY WAGTAIL

Little trotty wagtail, he went in the rain,
And tittering, tottering sideways he ne'er got straight again,
He stooped to get a worm, and looked up to catch a fly,
And then he flew away ere his feathers they were dry.

Little trotty wagtail, he waddled in the mud,
And left his little footmarks, trample where he would.
He waddled in the water-pudge, and waggle went his tail,
And chirrupt up his wings to dry upon the garden rail.

Little trotty wagtail, you nimble all about,
And in the dimpling water-pudge you waddle in and out;
Your home is nigh at hand, and in the warm pigsty,
So, little Master Wagtail, I'll bid you a good-bye.
                                        John Clare

THE OWL

When cats run home and light is come,
    And dew is cold upon the ground,
And the far-off stream is dumb,
    And the whirring sail goes round,
    And the whirring sail goes round;
        Alone and warming his five wits,
        The white owl in the belfry sits.

When merry milkmaids click the latch,
    And rarely smells the new-mown hay,
And the cock hath sung beneath the thatch
    Twice or thrice his roundelay,
    Twice or thrice his roundelay;
        Alone and warming his five wits,
        The white owl in the belfry sits

        Alfred, Lord Tennyson

The common cormorant or shag
Lays eggs inside a paper bag.
The reason you will see no doubt
It is to keep the lightning out.
But what these unobservant birds
Have never noticed is that herds
Of wandering bears may come with buns
And steal the bags to hold the crumbs.
                                        Anon

FOUR DUCKS ON A POND

Four ducks on a pond,
A grass-bank beyond,
A blue sky of spring,
White clouds on the wing:
What a little thing
To remember for years –
To remember with tears!
                    William Allingham

THE EAGLE

He clasps the crag with crooked hands;
Close to the sun in lonely lands,
Ring'd with the azure world, he stands.

The wrinkled sea beneath him crawls;
He watches from his mountain walls,
And like a thunderbolt he falls.
                    Alfred, Lord Tennyson

THE THRUSH'S NEST

Within a thick and spreading hawthorn bush,
That overhung a mole-hill large and round,
I heard from morn to morn a merry thrush
Sing hymns to sunrise, and I drank the sound
With joy; and, often an intruding guest,
I watched her secret toils from day to day –
How true she warped the moss to form a nest,
And modelled it within with wood and clay;
And by and by, like heath-bells gilt with dew,
There lay her shining eggs, as bright as flowers,
Ink-spotted over shells of greeny blue;
And there I witnessed, in the sunny hours
A brood of nature's minstrels chirp and fly,
Glad as that sunshine and the laughing sky.

John Clare

WHAT BIRD SO SINGS

What bird so sings, yet so does wail?
Oh! 'tis the ravished nightingale.
Jug, jug, jug, jug, tereu! she cries,
And still her woes at midnight rise.
Brave prick-song! who is't now we hear?
None but the lark so shrill and clear;
How at heaven's gates she claps her wings! –
The morn not waking till she sings.
Hark, hark, with what a pretty throat
Poor Robin Redbreast tunes his note;
Hark how the jolly cuckoos sing
Cuckoo! to welcome in the spring!
Cuckoo! to welcome in the spring!

John Lyly

ANSWER TO A CHILD'S QUESTION

Do you ask what the birds say? The Sparrow, the Dove,
The Linnet and Thrush say, "I love and I love!"
In the winter they're silent – the wind is so strong;
What it says, I don't know, but it sings a loud song.
But green leaves, and blossoms, and sunny warm weather,
And singing, and loving – all come back together.
But the Lark is so brimful of gladness and love,
The green fields below him, the blue sky above,
That he sings, and he sings: and for ever sings he –
"I love my Love, and my Love loves me!"

Samuel Taylor Coleridge

A STORY I'LL TO YOU UNFOLD

THE BABES IN THE WOOD

My dear, do you know
How a long time ago,
   Two poor little children,
Whose names I don't know,
Were stolen away
On a fine summer's day,
   And left in a wood,
As I've heard people say.

And when it was night,
So sad was their plight,
   The sun it went down,
And the moon gave no light!
They sobbed and they sighed,
And they bitterly cried,
   And the poor little things,
They lay down and died.

And when they were dead,
The robins so red
   Brought strawberry leaves
And over them spread;
And all the day long,
They sang them this song –
   Poor babes in the wood!
   Poor babes in the wood!
And won't you remember
   The babes in the wood?

Anon

THE GIPSY LADDIE

It was late in the night when the Squire came home
Enquiring for his lady.
His servant made a sure reply:
She's gone with the gipsum Davy.
   Rattle tum a gipsum gipsum
   Rattle tum a gipsum Davy.

O go catch up my milk-white steed,
The black one's not so speedy,
I'll ride all night till broad daylight,
Or overtake my lady.

He rode and he rode till he came to the town,
He rode till he came to Barley.
The tears came rolling down his cheeks,
And then he spied his lady.

It's come go back, my dearest dear,
Come go back, my honey;
It's come go back, my dearest dear,
And you never shall lack for money.

I won't go back, my dearest dear,
I won't go back, my honey;
For I wouldn't give a kiss from gipsum's lips
For you and all your money.

It's go pull off those snow-white gloves,
A-made of Spanish leather,
And give to me your lily-white hand,
And bid farewell for ever.

It's she pulled off those snow-white gloves,
A-made of Spanish leather,
And gave to him her lily-white hand,
And bade farewell for ever.

She soon ran through her gay clothing,
Her velvet shoes and stockings;
Her gold ring off her finger's gone,
And the gold plate off her bosom.

O once I had a house and land,
Feather-bed and money;
But now I've come to an old straw pad
With the gipsies dancing round me.

Anon

LITTLE BILLEE

There were three sailors of Bristol city
Who took a boat and went to sea.
But first with beef and captain's biscuits
And pickled pork they loaded she.

There was gorging Jack and guzzling Jimmy,
And the youngest he was little Billee.
Now when they got as far as the Equator
They'd nothing left but one split pea.

Says gorging Jack to guzzling Jimmy,
"I am extremely hungaree."
To gorging Jack says guzzling Jimmy,
"We've nothing left, us must eat we."

Says gorging Jack to guzzling Jimmy,
"With one another we shouldn't agree!
There's little Bill, he's young and tender,
We're old and tough, so let's eat he."

"Oh! Billy, we're going to kill and eat you,
So undo the button of your chemie."
When Bill received this information
He used his pocket handkerchie.

"First let me say my catechism,
Which my poor mammy taught to me."
"Make haste, make haste," says guzzling Jimmy,
While Jack pulled out his snickersnee.

So Billy went up to the main-top gallant mast,
And down he fell on his bended knee.
He scarce had come to the twelfth commandment
When up he jumps, "There's land I see:

"Jerusalem and Madagascar,
And North and South Amerikee:
There's the British flag a–riding at anchor,
With Admiral Napier, K.C.B."

So when they got aboard of the Admiral's,
He hanged fat Jack and flogged Jimmee;
But as for little Bill he made him
The Captain of a Seventy-three.

W. M. Thackeray

ROBIN HOOD AND THE BISHOP OF HEREFORD

Come, Gentlemen all, and listen a while;
A story I'll to you unfold –
How Robin Hood served the Bishop,
When he robb'd him of his gold.

As it befell in merry Barnsdale,
And under the green-wood tree,
The Bishop of Hereford was to come by,
With all his companye.

"Come, kill a ven'son," said bold Robin Hood,
"Come, kill me a good fat deer;
The Bishop's to dine with me today,
And he shall pay well for his cheer.

"We'll kill a fat ven'son," said bold Robin Hood,
"And dress't by the highway-side,
And narrowly watch for the Bishop,
Lest some other way he should ride."

He dress'd himself up in shepherd's attire,
With six of his men also;
And the Bishop of Hereford came thereby,
As about the fire they did go.

"What matter is this?" said the Bishop;
"Or for whom do you make this a-do?
Or why do you kill the King's ven'son,
When your company is so few?"

"We are shepherds," said bold Robin Hood,
"And we keep sheep all the year;
And we are disposed to be merry this day,
And to kill of the King's fat deer."

"You are brave fellowes," said the Bishop,
"And the King of your doings shall know;
Therefore make haste, come along with me,
For before the King you shall go."

"O pardon, O pardon," says bold Robin Hood,
"O pardon, I thee pray!
For it never becomes your lordship's coat
To take so many lives away."

"No pardon, no pardon!" the Bishop says;
"No pardon I thee owe;
Therefore make haste, come along with me,
For before the King you shall go."

Robin set his back against a tree,
And his foot against a thorn,
And from underneath his shepherd's coat,
He pull'd out a bugle horn.

He put the little end to his mouth,
And a loud blast he did blow,
Till threescore and ten of Robin's bold men,
Came running all on a row;

All making obeisance to bold Robin Hood;
'Twas a comely sight for to see;
"What matter, my master," said Little
                                                    John,
"That you blow so hastilye?" –

"O here is the Bishop of Hereford,
And no pardon we shall have." –
"Cut off his head, master," said Little
                                                    John,
"And throw him into his grave." –

74

"O pardon, O pardon," said the Bishop,
"O pardon, I thee pray!
For if I had known it had been you,
I'd have gone some other way." –

"No pardon, no pardon!" said Robin Hood;
"No pardon I thee owe;
Therefore make haste, come along with me,
For to merry Barnsdale you shall go."

Then Robin has taken the Bishop's hand
And led him to merry Barnsdale;
He made him to stay and sup with him that night,
And to drink wine, beer and ale.

"Call in the reckoning," said the Bishop,
"For methinks it grows wondrous high," –
"Lend me your purse, Bishop," said Little John,
"And I'll tell you by-and-by."

Then Little John took the Bishop's cloak,
And spread it upon the ground,
And out of the Bishop's portmanteau
He told three hundred pound.

"So now let him go," said Robin Hood.
Said Little John, "That may not be;
For I vow and protest he shall sing us a mass
Before that he go from me."

Robin Hood took the Bishop by the hand,
And bound him fast to a tree,
And made him to sing a mass, God wot,
To him and his yeomandrye.

Then Robin Hood brought him through the wood
And caused the music to play,
And he made the Bishop to dance in his boots,
And they set him on 's dapple-grey,
And they gave the tail within his hand –
And glad he could so get away.

Anon

CASEY JONES

Come all you rounders if you want to hear
The story of a brave engineer;
Casey Jones was the hogger's name,
On a big eight-wheeler, boys, he won his fame.
Caller called Casey at half-past four,
He kissed his wife at the station door,
Mounted to the cabin with orders in his hand,
And took his farewell trip to the promised land.

   Casey Jones, he mounted to the cabin,
   Casey Jones, with his orders in his hand!
   Casey Jones, he mounted to the cabin,
   Took his farewell trip into the promised land.

"Put in your water and shovel in your coal,
Put your head out the window, watch the drivers roll,
I'll run her till she leaves the rail,
'Cause we're eight hours late with the Western Mail!"
He looked at his watch and his watch was slow,
Looked at the water and the water was low,
Turned to his fireboy and said,
"We'll get to 'Frisco, but we'll all be dead!"

   Casey Jones, he mounted to the cabin,
   Casey Jones, with his orders in his hand!
   Casey Jones, he mounted to the cabin,
   Took his farewell trip into the promised land.

Casey pulled up Reno Hill,
Tooted for the crossing with an awful shrill,
Snakes all knew by the engine's moans
That the hogger at the throttle was Casey Jones.
He pulled up short two miles from the place,
Number Four stared him right in the face,
Turned to his fireboy, said, "You'd better jump,
'Cause there's two locomotives that's going to bump."

Casey Jones, he mounted to the cabin,
Casey Jones, with his orders in his hand!
Casey Jones, he mounted to the cabin,
Took his farewell trip into the promised land.

Casey said, just before he died,
"There's two more roads I'd like to ride."
Fireboy said, "What can they be?"
"The Rio Grande and the Old S.P."
Mrs. Jones sat on her bed a-sighing,
Got a pink that Casey was dying.
Said, "Go to bed, children; hush your crying,
'Cause you'll get another papa on the Salt Lake line."

Casey Jones! Got another papa!
Casey Jones, on the Salt Lake Line!
Casey Jones! Got another papa!
Got another papa on the Salt Lake Line!

Anon

FLANNAN ISLE

'Though three men dwell on Flannan Isle
To keep the lamp alight,
As we steered under the lee, we caught
No glimmer through the night.'

A passing ship at dawn had brought
The news, and quickly we set sail,
To find out what strange thing might ail
The keepers of the deep-sea light.

The winter day broke blue and bright
With glancing sun and glancing spray
While o'er the swell our boat made way,
As gallant as a gull in flight.

But as we neared the lonely Isle
And looked up at the naked height,
And saw the lighthouse towering white
With blinded lantern, that all night
Had never shot a spark
Of comfort through the dark,
So ghostly in the cold sunlight
It seemed that we were struck the while
With wonder all too dread for words.

And, as into the tiny creek
We stole beneath the hanging crag,
We saw three queer black ugly birds –
Too big by far in my belief,
For cormorant or shag –
Like seamen sitting bolt-upright
Up on a half-tide reef:
But, as we neared, they plunged from sight
Without a sound or spurt of white.

And still too mazed to speak,
We landed; and made fast the boat;
And climbed the track in single file,
Each wishing he was safe afloat
On any sea, however far,
So it be far from Flannan Isle:

And still we seemed to climb and climb
As though we'd lost all count of time
And so must climb for evermore.
Yet, all too soon, we reached the door –
The black, sun-blistered lighthouse-door,
That gaped for us ajar.

As, on the threshold, for a spell
We paused, we seemed to breathe the smell
Of limewash and of tar,
Familiar as our daily breath,
As though 'twere some strange scent of death;
And so yet wondering, side by side
We stood a moment still tongue-tied;
And each with black foreboding eyed
The door, ere we should fling it wide
To leave the sunlight for the gloom:
Till, plucking courage up, at last
Hard on each other's heels we passed
Into the living-room.

Yet, as we crowded through the door
We only saw a table, spread
For dinner, meat and cheese and bread;
But all untouched; and no one there:
As though, when they sat down to eat,
Ere they could even taste,
Alarm had come; and they in haste
Had risen and left the bread and meat,
For at the table-head a chair
Lay tumbled on the floor.

We listened, but we only heard
The feeble chirping of a bird
That starved upon its perch;
And, listening still, without a word
We set about our hopeless search.
We hunted high, we hunted low,
And soon ransacked the empty house;
Then o'er the Island, to and fro
We ranged, to listen and to look
In every cranny, cleft or nook
That might have hid a bird or mouse:

But though we searched from shore to shore
We found no sign in any place,
And soon again stood face to face
Before the gaping door,
And stole into the room once more
As frightened children steal.

Ay, though we hunted high and low
And hunted everywhere,
Of the three men's fate we found no trace
Of any kind in any place
But a door ajar, and an untouched meal,
And an overtoppled chair.

And as we listened in the gloom
Of that forsaken living-room –
A chill clutch on our breath –
We thought how ill-chance came to all
Who kept the Flannan Light,
And how the rock had been the death
Of many a likely lad –
How six had come to a sudden end
And three had gone stark mad,
And one whom we'd all known as friend,
Had leapt from the lantern one still night,
And fallen dead by the lighthouse wall –
And long we thought
On the three we sought,
And on what might yet befall.

Like curs a glance has brought to heel
We listened, flinching there,
And looked, and looked, on the untouched meal,
And the overtoppled chair.

We seemed to stand for an endless while,
Though still no word was said,
Three men alive on Flannan Isle
Who thought on three men dead.

                                   Wilfrid Wilson Gibson

THE BALLAD OF SEMMERWATER

Deep asleep, deep asleep,
Deep asleep it lies,
The still lake of Semmerwater
Under the still skies.

And many a fathom, many a fathom,
Many a fathom below,
In a kings' tower and a queen's bower
The fishes come and go.

Once there stood by Semmerwater
A mickle town and tall;
King's tower and queen's bower,
And wakeman on the wall.

Came a beggar halt and sore:
"I faint for lack of bread."
King's tower and queen's bower
Cast him forth unfed.

He knocked at the door of the herdsman's cot,
The herdsman's cot in the dale.
They gave him of their oatcake,
They gave him of their ale.

He has cursed aloud that city proud,
He has cursed it in its pride;
He has cursed it into Semmerwater
Down the brant hillside;
He has cursed it into Semmerwater
There to bide.

King's tower and queen's bower,
And a mickle town and tall;
By glimmer of scale and gleam of fin,
Folk have seen them all.
King's tower and queen's bower,
And weed and reed in the gloom;
And a lost city in Semmerwater,
Deep asleep till Doom.

William Watson

O'ER DITCHES AND MIRES

MEET-ON-THE-ROAD

"Now, pray, where are you going?" said Meet-on-the-Road.
"To school, sir, to school, sir," said Child-as-it-Stood.

"What have you in your basket, child?" said Meet-on-the-Road.
"My dinner, sir, my dinner, sir," said Child-as-it-Stood.

"What have you for dinner, child?" said Meet-on-the-Road.
"Some pudding, sir, some pudding, sir," said Child-as-it-Stood.

"Oh, then, I pray, give me a share," said Meet-on-the-Road.
"I've little enough for myself, sir," said Child-as-it-Stood.

"What have you got that cloak on for?" said Meet-on-the-Road.
"To keep the wind and cold from me," said Child-as-it-Stood.

"I wish the wind would blow through you," said Meet-on-the-Road.
"Oh, what a wish! What a wish!" said Child-as-it-Stood.

"Pray, what are those bells ringing for?" said Meet-on-the-Road.
"To ring bad spirits home again," said Child-as-it-Stood.

"Oh, then I must be going, child!" said Meet-on-the-Road.
"So fare you well, so fare you well," said Child-as-it-Stood.

Anon

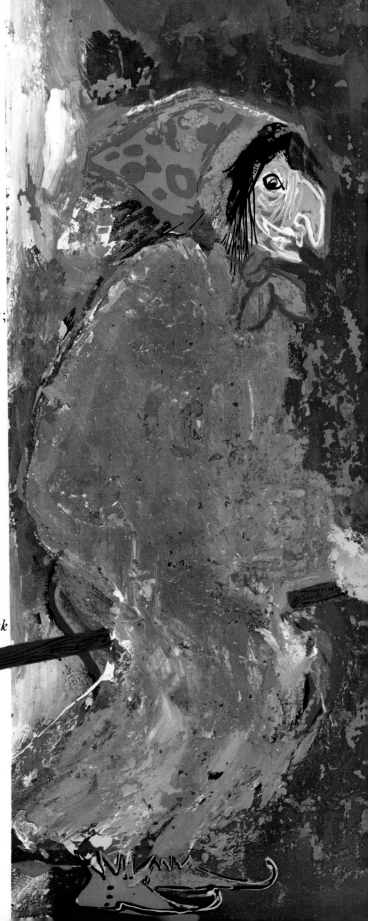

THE HAG

The Hag is astride,
  This night for to ride;
The Devil and she together;
  Through thick and through thin,
  Now out and then in,
Though ne'er so foul be the weather.

A thorn or a burr
  She takes for a spur,
With a lash of a bramble she rides now;
  Through brakes and through briars,
  O'er ditches and mires,
She follows the Spirit that guides now.

No beast, for his food
  Dares now range the wood,
But hushed in his lair he lies lurking;
  While mischiefs, by these,
  On land and on seas,
At noon of night are a–working.

The storm will arise
  And trouble the skies;
This night, and more for the wonder,
  The ghost from the tomb
  Affrighted shall come,
Called out by the clap of the thunder.
            Robert Herrick

A wife was sitting at her reel ae night;
  And aye she sat, and aye she reeled, and aye she
    wished for company.

In came a pair o' braid braid soles, and sat down
      at the fireside;
  And aye she sat, and aye she reeled, and aye she
    wished for company.

In came a pair o' sma' sma' legs, and sat down on the
      braid braid soles;
  And aye she sat, and aye she reeled, and aye she
    wished for company.

In came a pair o' muckle muckle knees, and sat down
      on the sma' sma' legs;
  And aye she sat, and aye she reeled, and aye she
    wished for company.

In came a pair o' sma' sma' thees, and sat down on
      the muckle muckle knees;
  And aye she sat, and aye she reeled, and aye she
    wished for company.

In came a pair o' muckle muckle hips, and sat down on
      the sma' sma' thees;
  And aye she sat, and aye she reeled, and aye she
    wished for company.

In came a sma' sma' waist, and sat down on the
      muckle muckle hips;
  And aye she sat, and aye she reeled, and aye she
    wished for company.

In came a pair o' braid braid shouthers, and sat down
      on the sma' sma' waist;
  And aye she sat, and aye she reeled, and aye she
    wished for company.

In came a pair o' sma' sma' arms, and sat down on
      the braid braid shouthers;
  And aye she sat, and aye she reeled, and aye she
    wished for company.

In came a pair o' muckle muckle hands, and sat down
    on the sma' sma' arms;
  And aye she sat, and aye she reeled, and aye she
    wished for company.

In came a sma' sma' neck, and sat down on the braid
    braid shouthers;
  And aye she sat, and aye she reeled, and aye she
    wished for company.

In came a great big head, and sat down on the sma'
    sma' neck;
  And aye she sat, and aye she reeled, and aye she
    wished for company.

"What way hae ye sic braid braid feet?" quo' the wife.
"Muckle ganging, muckle ganging."
"What way hae ye sic sma' sma' legs?"
"*Aih-h-h!* – late – and *wee-e-e* moul."
"What way hae ye sic muckle muckle knees?"
"Muckle praying, muckle praying."
"What way hae ye sic sma' sma' thees?"
"*Aih-h-h!* – late – and *wee-e-e* moul."
"What way hae ye sic big big hips?"
"Muckle sitting, muckle sitting."
"What way hae ye sic a sma' sma' waist?"
"*Aih-h-h!* – late – and *wee-e-e* moul."
"What way hae ye sic braid braid shouthers?"
"Wi' carrying broom, wi' carrying broom."
"What way hae ye sic sma' sma' arms?"
"*Aih-h-h!* – late – and *wee-e-e* moul."
"What way hae ye sic muckle muckle hands?"
"Threshing wi' an iron flail, threshing wi' an iron flail."
"What way hae ye sic a sma' sma' neck?"
"*Aih-h-h!* – late – and *wee-e-e* moul."
"What way hae ye sic a muckle muckle head?"
"Muckle wit, muckle wit."
"What do you come for?"
"For YOU!"

Anon

reel, a frame for winding yarn; *ae*, one;
braid, broad; *thees*, thighs; *muckle*, big; *shouthers*, shoulders.
sic, such; *muckle ganging*, much walking.

AT THE KEYHOLE

"Grill me some bones," said the Cobbler,
  "Some bones, my pretty Sue;
I'm tired of my lonesome with heels and soles,
Springsides and uppers too;
A mouse in the wainscot is nibbling;
A wind in the keyhole drones;
And a sheet webbed over my candle, Susie, –
  Grill me some bones!"

"Grill me some bones," said the Cobbler,
  "I sat at my tic-tac-to;
And a footstep came to my door and stopped,
And a hand groped to and fro;
And I peered up over my boot and last;
And my feet went cold as stones: –
I saw an eye at the keyhole, Susie! –
  Grill me some bones!"

Walter de la Mare

WITCHES' CHARM

The owl is abroad, the bat and the toad,
  And so is the cat-a-mountain;
The ant and the mole both sit in a hole,
  And frog peeps out o' the fountain.
The dogs they do bay, and the timbrels play,
  The spindle is now a-turning;
The moon it is red, and the stars are fled,
  But all the sky is a-burning:
The ditch is made, and our nails the spade:
With pictures full, of wax and wool,
Their livers I stick with needles quick;
There lacks but the blood to make up the flood.
Quickly, dame, then bring your part in!
Spur, spur, upon little Martin!
Merrily, merrily, make him sail,
A worm in his mouth and a thorn in's tail,
Fire above, and fire below,
With a whip i' your hand to make him go!

Ben Jonson

SWEET SPRITES

THE FAIRIES

If ye will with Mab find grace,
Let each platter in his place;
Rake the fire up, and get
Water in, ere sun be set;
Wash your pails, and cleanse your dairies,
Sluts are loathsome to the fairies.
Sweep your house; who doth not so,
Mab will pinch her by the toe.

Robert Herrick

ARIEL'S SONG

Come unto these yellow sands,
    And then take hands:
Curtsied when you have, and kiss'd –
    The wild waves whist;
Foot it featly here and there;
And, sweet sprites, the burden bear.
    Hark, hark!
        Bow-wow
    The watch-dogs bark:
        Bow-wow,
    Hark, hark! I hear
    The strain of strutting Chanticleer
    Cry, Cock-a-diddle-dow.

William Shakespeare

OVER HILL, OVER DALE

Over hill, over dale,
    Thorough bush, thorough brier,
Over park, over pale,
    Thorough flood, thorough fire:
I do wander everywhere,
Swifter than the moones sphere;
And I serve the fairy queen,
To dew her orbs upon the green.
The cowslips tall her pensioners be;
In their gold coats spots you see;
Those be rubies, fairy favours,
In those freckles live their savours:
I must go seek some dew-drops here,
And hang a pearl in every cowslip's ear.

William Shakespeare

THE SONG OF WANDERING AENGUS

I went out to the hazel wood,
Because a fire was in my head,
And cut and peeled a hazel wand,
And hooked a berry to a thread;
And when white moths were on the wing,
And moth-like stars were flickering out,
I dropped the berry in a stream,
And caught a little silver trout.

When I had laid it on the floor
I went to blow the fire aflame,
But something rustled on the floor,
And someone called me by my name;
It had become a glimmering girl
With apple blossom in her hair
Who called me by my name and ran
And faded through the brightening air.

Though I am old with wandering
Through hollow lands and hilly lands,
I will find out where she has gone,
And kiss her lips and take her hands;
And walk among long dappled grass,
And pluck till time and times are done
The silver apples of the moon,
The golden apples of the sun.

W. B. Yeats

WHERE THE BEE SUCKS

Where the bee sucks, there suck I,
In a cowslip's bell I lie,
There I couch when owls do cry.
On the bat's back I do fly
After summer merrily.
Merrily, merrily shall I live now
Under the blossom that hangs on the bough.
William Shakespeare

THE FAIRIES

Up the airy mountain,
　Down the rushy glen,
We daren't go a-hunting
　For fear of little men;
Wee folk, good folk,
　Trooping all together;
Green jacket, red cap,
　And white owl's feather.

Down along the rocky shore
　Some make their home –
They live on crispy pancakes
　Of yellow tide-foam;
Some in the reeds
　Of the black mountain lake,
With frogs for their watch-dogs,
　All night awake.

High on the hill-top
　The old King sits;
He is now so old and grey
　He's nigh lost his wits.
With a bridge of white mist
　Columbkill he crosses,
On his stately journeys
　From Slieveleague to Rosses;
Or going up with music
　On cold starry nights,
To sup with the Queen
　Of the gay Northern Lights.

They stole little Bridget
  For seven years long;
When she came down again
  Her friends were all gone.
They took her lightly back,
  Between the night and morrow,
They thought that she was fast asleep,
  But she was dead with sorrow.
They have kept her ever since
  Deep within the lake,
On a bed of flag-leaves,
  Watching till she wake.

By the craggy hill-side,
  Through the mosses bare,
They have planted thorn-trees
  For pleasure here and there.
Is any man so daring
  As dig them up in spite,
He shall find their sharpest thorns
  In his bed at night.

Up the airy mountain,
  Down the rushy glen,
We daren't go a-hunting
  For fear of little men;
Wee folk, good folk,
  Trooping all together;
Green jacket, red cap,
  And white owl's feather!
     William Allingham

Hark! hark! the lark at heaven's gate sings,
　And Phoebus 'gins arise,
His steeds to water at those springs
　On chaliced flowers that lies;
And winking Mary-buds begin
　To ope their golden eyes;
With every thing that pretty is,
　My lady sweet, arise!
　　Arise, arise!
　　　　　　　William Shakespeare

COME WIND, COME WEATHER

A widow bird sate mourning for her love
   Upon a wintry bough;
The frozen wind crept on above,
   The freezing stream below.

There was no leaf upon the forest bare,
   No flower upon the ground,
And little motion in the air
   Except the mill-wheel's sound.

P. B. Shelley

WHO HAS SEEN THE WIND?

Who has seen the wind?
   Neither I nor you;
But when the leaves hang trembling
   The wind is passing through.

Who has seen the wind?
   Neither you nor I:
But when the trees bow down their heads
   The wind is passing by.

Christina Rossetti

WEATHERS

This is the weather the cuckoo likes,
   And so do I;
When showers betumble the chestnut spikes,
   And nestlings fly:
And the little brown nightingale bills his best,
And they sit outside at *The Traveller's Rest,*
And maids come forth sprig-muslin drest,
And citizens dream of the south and west,
   And so do I.

This is the weather the shepherd shuns,
   And so do I:
When beeches drip in browns and duns,
   And thresh, and ply;
And hill-hid tides throb, throe on throe,
And meadow rivulets overflow,
And drops on gate-bars hang in a row,
And rooks in families homeward go,
   And so do I.

Thomas Hardy

THE NORTH WIND DOTH BLOW

The north wind doth blow,
And we shall have snow,
And what will the robin do then, poor thing?
  He'll sit in a barn,
  And keep himself warm,
And hide his head under his wing, poor thing!

The north wind doth blow,
And we shall have snow,
And what will the swallow do then, poor thing?
  Oh, do you not know
  That he's off long ago,
To a country where he will find spring, poor thing!

The north wind doth blow,
And we shall have snow,
And what will the dormouse do then, poor thing?
  Roll'd up like a ball,
  In his nest snug and small,
He'll sleep till warm weather comes in, poor thing!

The north wind doth blow,
And we shall have snow,
And what will the honey-bee do then, poor thing?
  In his hive he will stay
  Till the cold is away,
And then he'll come out in the spring, poor thing!

The north wind doth blow,
And we shall have snow,
And what will the children do then, poor things?
  When lessons are done,
  They must skip, jump and run,
Until they have made themselves warm, poor things!

Anon

Up in the morning's no' for me,
   Up in the morning early;
When a' the hills are covered wi' snaw
   I'm sure it's winter fairly.

Cauld blaws the wind frae east to west,
   The drift is driving sairly;
Sae loud and shrill's I hear the blast,
   I'm sure it's winter fairly.

The birds sit chittering in the thorn,
   A' day they fare but sparely;
And long's the night frae e'en to morn;
   I'm sure it's winter fairly.

Robert Burns

WINTER

When icicles hang by the wall,
   And Dick the shepherd blows his nail,
And Tom bears logs into the hall,
   And milk comes frozen home in pail;
When blood is nipped, and ways be foul
Then nightly sings the staring owl
         Tu-who;
   Tu-whit, tu-who – a merry note,
   While greasy Joan doth keel the pot.

When all aloud the wind doth blow,
   And coughing drowns the parson's saw,
And birds sit brooding in the snow,
   And Marian's nose looks red and raw,
When roasted crabs hiss in the bowl,
Then nightly sings the staring owl
         Tu-who;
   Tu-whit, tu-who – a merry note,
   While greasy Joan doth keel the pot.

William Shakespeare

WINTER, THE HUNTSMAN

Through his iron glades
Rides Winter the Huntsman.
All colour fades
As his horn is heard sighing.

Far through the forest
His wild hooves crash and thunder
Till many a mighty branch
Is torn asunder.

As the red reynard creeps
To his hole near the river,
The copper leaves fall
And the bare trees shiver.

As night creeps from the ground,
Hides each tree from its brother,
And each dying sound
Reveals yet another.

Is it Winter the Huntsman
Who gallops through his iron glades,
Cracking his cruel whip
To the gathering shades?

Osbert Sitwell

NO!

No sun – no moon!
No morn – no noon –
No dawn – no dusk – no proper time of day –
No sky – no earthly view –
No distance looking blue –
No road – no street – no 't'other side the way' –
No end to any Row –
No indications where the Crescents go –
No top to any steeple –
No recognitions of familiar people –
No courtesies for showing 'em –
No knowing 'em! –
No travelling at all – no locomotion,
No inkling of the way – no notion –
'No go' – by land or ocean –
No mail – no post –
No news from any foreign coast –
No Park – no Ring – no afternoon gentility –
No company – no nobility –
No warmth, no cheerfulness, no healthful ease,
No comfortable feel in any member –
No shade, no shine, no butterflies, no bees,
No fruits, no flowers, no leaves, no birds, –
November!

Thomas Hood

ADDRESS TO A CHILD
DURING A BOISTEROUS WINTER EVENING

What way does the Wind come? What way does he go?
He rides over the water, and over the snow,
Through wood and through vale; and o'er rocky height
Which the goat cannot climb, takes his sounding flight;
   He tosses about in every bare tree,
   As, if you look up, you plainly may see;
But how he will come, and whither he goes,
There's never a scholar in England knows.

He will suddenly stop in a cunning nook,
And ring a sharp 'larum – but if you should look,
There's nothing to see but a cushion of snow
   Round as a pillow, and whiter than milk,
   And softer than if it were covered with silk.
Sometimes he'll hide in the cave of a rock,
Then whistle as shrill as the buzzard cock;
   Yet seek him – and what shall you find in the place?
   Nothing but silence and empty space;
Save, in a corner, a heap of dry leaves,
That he's left for a bed, to beggars or thieves.

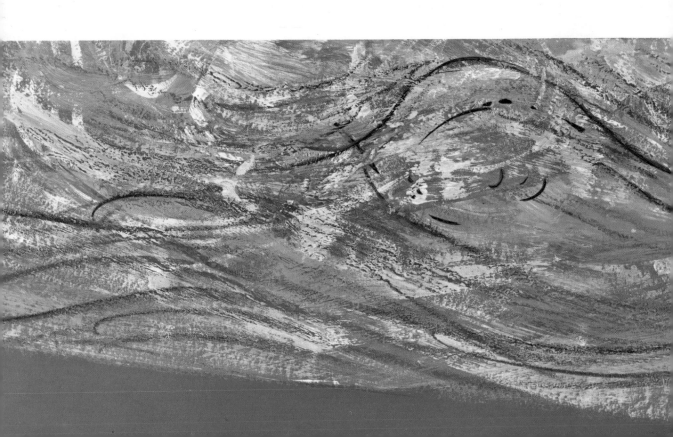

As soon as 'tis daylight tomorrow, with me
You shall go to the orchard, and then you will see
That he has been there, and made a great rout,
And cracked the branches, and strewn them about;
   Heaven grant that he spare but that one upright twig
   That looked up at the sky so proud and so big
All last summer, as well you know,
Studded with apples, a beautiful show!

Hark! over the roof he makes a pause,
And growls as if he would fix his claws
Right in the slates, and with a huge rattle
Drive them down, like men in a battle;
   But let him range round: he does us no harm,
   We build up the fire; we're snug and warm,
Untouched by his breath see the candle shines bright,
And burns with a clear and steady light;
Books have we to read – but that half-stifled knell,
Alas, 'tis the sound of the eight o'clock bell.

Come now we'll to bed! And when we are there
He may work at his own will, and what shall we care?
He may knock at the door – we'll not let him in;
May drive at the windows – we'll laugh at his din.
Let him seek his own home wherever it be;
Here's a cosy warm house for Edward and me.
Dorothy Wordsworth

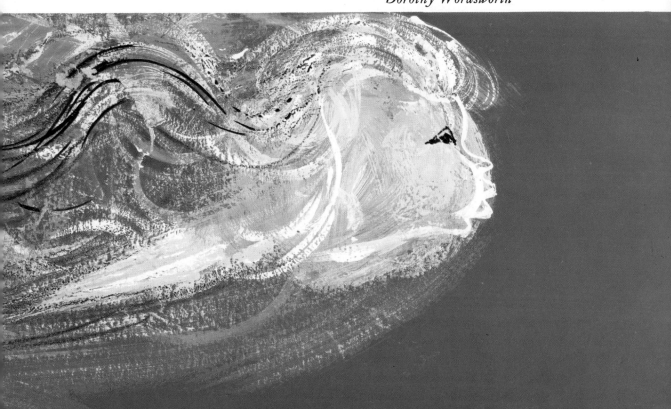

SPRING

Spring, the sweet Spring, is the year's pleasant king;
Then blooms each thing; then maids dance in a ring,
Cold doth not sting, the pretty birds do sing:
   Cuckoo, jug-jug, pu-we, to-witta-woo!

The palm and may make country houses gay,
Lambs frisk and play, the shepherds pipe all day,
And we hear aye birds tune this merry lay:
   Cuckoo, jug-jug, pu-we, to-witta-woo!

The fields breathe sweet, the daisies kiss our feet,
Young lovers meet, old wives a-sunning sit;
In every street these tunes our ears do greet:
   Cuckoo, jug-jug, pu-we, to-witta-woo!
     Spring, the sweet Spring!

Thomas Nashe

Here we come a-piping
In spring-time and in May;
Green fruit a-ripening,
And winter fled away.
The Queen she sits upon the strand,
Fair as a lily, white as wand;
Seven billows on the sea,
Horses riding fast and free,
And bells beyond the sand.

Anon

HE IS OF THE TRIBE OF TIGER

CAT!

Cat!
Scat!
Atter her, atter her,
Sleeky flatterer,
Spitfire chatterer,
Scatter her, scatter her
  Off her mat!
  Wuff!
  Wuff!
  Treat her rough!
Git her, git her,
Whiskery spitter!
Catch her, catch her,
Green–eyed scratcher!
  Slathery
  Slithery
  Hisser,
  Don't miss her!
Run till you're dithery,
  Hithery
  Thithery
  Pfitts! pfitts!
  How she spits!
  Spitch! Spatch!
  Can't she scratch!
Scritching the bark
Of the sycamore–tree,
She's reached her ark
And's hissing at me
  Pfitts! Pfitts!
  Wuff! Wuff!
  Scat,
  Cat!
  That's
  That!

Eleanor Farjeon

There was a wee bit mousikie,
   That lived in Gilberaty-O,
It couldno' get a bite o' cheese,
   For Cheatie-Pussy-Catty-O.

It said unto the cheesiky,
   "Oh fain would I be at ye-O,
If 'twere no' for the cruel claws
   O' Cheatie-Pussy-Catty-O."
                              Anon

THE SONG OF THE JELLICLES

Jellicle Cats come out to-night,
Jellicle Cats come one come all :
The Jellicle Moon is shining bright—
Jellicles come to the Jellicle Ball.

Jellicle Cats are black and white,
Jellicle Cats are rather small;
Jellicle Cats are merry and bright,
And pleasant to hear when they caterwaul.
Jellicle Cats have cheerful faces,
Jellicle Cats have bright black eyes;
They like to practise their airs and graces
And wait for the Jellicle Moon to rise.

Jellicle Cats develop slowly,
Jellicle Cats are not too big;
Jellicle Cats are roly-poly,
They know how to dance a gavotte and a jig.
Until the Jellicle Moon appears
They make their toilette and take their repose:
Jellicles wash behind their ears,
Jellicles dry between their toes.

Jellicle Cats are white and black,
Jellicle Cats are of moderate size;
Jellicles jump like a jumping-jack,
Jellicle Cats have moonlit eyes.
They're quiet enough in the morning hours,
They're quiet enough in the afternoon,
Reserving their terpsichorean powers
To dance by the light of the Jellicle Moon.

Jellicle Cats are black and white,
Jellicle Cats (as I said) are small;
If it happens to be a stormy night
They will practise a caper or two in the hall.
If it happens the sun is shining bright
You would say they had nothing to do at all:
They are resting and saving themselves to be right
For the Jellicle Moon and the Jellicle Ball.

T. S. Eliot

THE KITTEN AND THE FALLING LEAVES

See the Kitten on the wall,
Sporting with the leaves that fall,
Withered leaves – one-two-and three –
From the lofty elder-tree!
Through the calm and frosty air
Of this morning bright and fair,
Eddying round and round they sink
Softly, slowly: one might think,
From the motions that are made,
Every little leaf conveyed
Sylph or Faery hither tending,
To this lower world descending,
Each invisible and mute
In his wavering parachute.

– But the Kitten, how she starts,
Crouches, stretches, paws, and darts!
First at one, and then its fellow
Just as light and just as yellow.
There are many now – now one –
Now they stop and there are none:

106

What intenseness of desire
In her upward eye of fire!
With a tiger-leap half-way
Now she meets the coming prey,
Lets it go as fast, and then
Has it in her power again:
Now she works with three or four,
Like an Indian conjurer;
Quick as he in feats of art,
Far beyond in joy of heart.
Were her antics played in the eye
Of a thousand standers-by,
Clapping hands with shout and stare,
What would little Tabby care
For the plaudits of the crowd?

William Wordsworth

MY CAT JEOFFRY

For I will consider my Cat Jeoffry.
For he is the servant of the Living God, duly and daily
serving him.
For at the first glance of the glory of God in the East
he worships in his way.
For is this done by wreathing his body seven times
round with elegant quickness.
For then he leaps up to catch the musk, which is the
blessing of God upon his prayer.
For he rolls upon prank to work it in.
For having done duty and received blessing he begins to
consider himself.
For this he performs in ten degrees.
For first he looks upon his fore-paws to see if they are
clean.
For secondly he kicks up behind to clear away there.
For thirdly he works it upon stretch with the fore-paws
extended.
For fourthly he sharpens his paws by wood.
For fifthly he washes himself.
For sixthly he rolls upon wash.

For seventhly he fleas himself, that he may not be
        interrupted upon the beat.
For eighthly he rubs himself against a post.
For ninthly he looks up for his instructions.
For tenthly he goes in quest of food.
For having consider'd God and himself he will consider
        his neighbour.
For if he meets another cat he will kiss her in kindness.
For when he takes his prey he plays with it to give it
        a chance.
For one mouse in seven escapes by his dallying.
For when his day's work is done his business
        more properly begins.
For he keeps the Lord's watch in the night against
        the adversary.
For he counteracts the powers of darkness by his
        electrical skin & glaring eyes.
For he counteracts the Devil, who is death, by
        brisking about the life.
For in his morning orisons he loves the sun and the
        sun loves him.
For he is of the tribe of Tiger.
For the Cherub Cat is a term of the Angel Tiger.
For he has the subtlety and hissing of a serpent,
        which in goodness he suppresses.
For he will not do destruction, if he is well-fed,
        neither will he spit without provocation.
For he purrs in thankfulness, when God tells him
        he's a good Cat.
For he is an instrument for the children to learn
        benevolence upon.
For every house is incompleat without him & a
        blessing is lacking in the spirit.
                                    Christopher Smart

A CAT

She had a name among the children;
But no one loved though someone owned
Her, locked her out of doors at bedtime
And had her kittens duly drowned.

In Spring, nevertheless, this cat
Ate blackbirds, thrushes, nightingales,
And birds of bright voice and plume and flight,
As well as scraps from neighbours' pails.

I loathed and hated her for this;
One speckle on a thrush's breast
Was worth a million such; and yet
She lived long, till God gave her rest.
Edward Thomas

THE CAT

Within that porch, across the way,
I see two naked eyes this night;
Two eyes that neither shut nor blink,
Searching my face with a green light.

But cats to me are strange, so strange –
I cannot sleep if one is near;
And though I'm sure I see those eyes,
I'm not so sure a body's there!
W. H. Davies

MILK FOR THE CAT

When the tea is brought at five o'clock,
And all the neat curtains are drawn with care,
The little black cat with bright green eyes
Is suddenly purring there.

At first she pretends, having nothing to do,
She has come in merely to blink by the grate,
But, though tea may be late or the milk may be sour,
She is never late.

And presently her agate eyes
Take a soft large milky haze,
And her independent casual glance
Becomes a stiff, hard gaze.

Then she stamps her claws or lifts her ears,
Or twists her tail and begins to stir,
Till suddenly all her lithe body becomes
One breathing, trembling purr.

The children eat and wriggle and laugh;
The two old ladies stroke their silk:
But the cat is grown small and thin with desire,
Transformed to a creeping lust for milk.

The white saucer like some full moon descends
At last from the clouds of the table above;
She sighs and dreams and thrills and glows,
Transfigured with love.

She nestles over the shining rim,
Buries her chin in the creamy sea;
Her tail hangs loose; each drowsy paw
Is doubled under each bending knee.

A long, dim ecstasy holds her life;
Her world is an infinite shapeless white,
Till her tongue has curled the last holy drop,
Then she sinks back into the night,

Draws and dips her body to heap
Her sleepy nerves in the great arm–chair,
Lies defeated and buried deep
Three or four hours unconscious there.
                                    Harold Monro

THE TYGER

Tyger! Tyger! burning bright
In the forests of the night,
What immortal hand or eye
Could frame thy fearful symmetry?

In what distant deeps or skies
Burnt the fire of thine eyes?
On what wings dare he aspire?
What the hand dare seize the fire?

And what shoulder, and what art,
Could twist the sinews of thy heart?
And when thy heart began to beat,
What dread hand? and what dread feet?

What the hammer? what the chain?
In what furnace was thy brain?
What the anvil? what dread grasp
Dare its deadly terrors clasp?

When the stars threw down their spears,
And water'd heaven with their tears,
Did he smile his work to see?
Did he who made the Lamb make thee?

Tyger! Tyger! burning bright
In the forests of the night,
What immortal hand or eye
Dare frame thy fearful symmetry?

William Blake

INDIA

They hunt, the velvet tigers in the jungle,
The spotted jungle full of shapeless patches –
Sometimes they're leaves, sometimes they're hanging flowers,
Sometimes they're hot gold patches of the sun:
They hunt, the velvet tigers in the jungle!

What do they hunt by glimmering pools of water,
By the round silver Moon, the Pool of Heaven –
In the striped grass, amid the barkless trees –
The stars scattered like eyes of beasts above them!

What do they hunt, their hot breath scorching insects,
Insects that blunder blindly in the way,
Vividly fluttering – they also are hunting,
Are glittering with a tiny ecstasy!

The grass is flaming and the trees are growing,
The very mud is gurgling in the pools,
Green toads are watching, crimson parrots flying,
Two pairs of eyes meet one another glowing –
They hunt, the velvet tigers in the jungle.

W. J. Turner

OTHER CREATURES

MISTER FOX

A fox went out in a hungry plight,
And he begged of the moon to give him light,
For he'd many miles to trot that night,
   Before he could reach his den O!

And first he came to a farmer's yard,
Where the ducks and geese declared it hard
That their nerves should be shaken and their rest be marr'd,
   By the visit of Mister Fox O!

He took the grey goose by the sleeve;
Says he, "Madam Goose, and by your leave,
I'll take you away without reprieve,
   And carry you home to my den O!"

He seized the black duck by the neck,
And swung her over across his back;
The black duck cried out, "Quack! Quack! Quack!"
   With her legs hanging dangling down O!

Then old Mrs. Slipper-Slopper jump'd out of bed,
And out of the window she popp'd her head,
Crying, "John, John, John, the grey goose is gone,
   And the fox is away to his den O!"

Then John he went up to the top of the hill,
And he blew a blast both loud and shrill;
Says the fox, "That is very pretty music – still
   I'd rather be in my den O!"

At last the fox got home to his den;
To his dear little foxes, eight, nine, ten,
Says he, "You're in luck, here's a good fat duck,
   With her legs hanging dangling down O!"

He then sat down with his hungry wife;
They did very well without fork or knife;
They'd never ate better in all their life,
   And the little ones pick'd the bones O!

Anon

A farmer's dog leaped over the stile,
His name was little Bingo;
There was B with an I, I with an N,
N with a G, G with an O,
There was B, I, N, G, O,
And his name was little Bingo.

Anon

JOHN COOK

John Cook he had a little grey mare,
  Hee, haw, hum;
Her legs were long and her back was bare,
  Hee, haw, hum;
John Cook was riding up Shooter's Bank,
  Hee, haw, hum;
The mare she began to kick and to prank,
  Hee, haw, hum;
John Cook was riding up Shooter's Hill,
  Hee, haw, hum;
His mare fell down and made her will,
  Hee, haw, hum;
The bridle and saddle were laid on the shelf,
  Hee, haw, hum;
If you want any more you may sing it yourself,
  Hee, haw, hum.   *Anon*

I had a little pony,
  His name was Dapple-grey.
I lent him to a lady,
  To ride a mile away.

She whipped him, she lashed him,
  She drove him through the mire.
I wouldn't lend my pony now,
  For all the lady's hire.

Anon

HOW DOTH THE LITTLE CROCODILE

How doth the little crocodile
  Improve his shining tail,
And pour the waters of the Nile
  On every golden scale!

How cheerfully he seems to grin,
  How neatly spreads his claws,
And welcomes little fishes in,
  With gently smiling jaws!
                              Lewis Carroll

THE COW

The friendly cow, all red and white,
  I love with all my heart:
She gives me cream with all her might,
  To eat with apple-tart.

She wanders lowing here and there,
  And yet she cannot stray,
All in the pleasant open air,
  The pleasant light of day;

And blown by all the winds that pass
  And wet with all the showers,
She walks among the meadow grass
  And eats the meadow flowers.
                              R. L. Stevenson

THE YAK

As a friend to the children commend me the Yak.
  You will find it exactly the thing:
It will carry and fetch, you can ride on its back,
  Or lead it about with a string.

The Tartar who dwells on the plains of Thibet
  (A desolate region of snow)
Has for centuries made it a nursery pet,
  And surely the Tartar should know!

Then tell your papa where the Yak can be got,
  And if he is awfully rich
He will buy you the creature – or else he will not.
  (I cannot be positive which.)

Hilaire Belloc

THE OWL AND THE PUSSY-CAT

The Owl and the Pussy-Cat went to sea
  In a beautiful pea-green boat,
They took some honey, and plenty of money,
  Wrapped up in a five-pound note.
The Owl looked up to the stars above,
  And sang to a small guitar,
"O lovely Pussy! O Pussy, my love,
  What a beautiful Pussy you are,
    You are,
    You are!
What a beautiful Pussy you are!"

Pussy said to the Owl, "You elegant fowl!
  How charmingly sweet you sing!
O let us be married! too long we have tarried:
  But what shall we do for a ring?"
They sailed away, for a year and a day,
  To the land where the Bong-Tree grows,
And there in a wood a Piggy-wig stood,
  With a ring at the end of his nose,
    His nose,
    His nose,
  With a ring at the end of his nose.

"Dear Pig, are you willing to sell for one shilling
    Your ring?" Said the Piggy, "I will."
So they took it away, and were married next day
    By the Turkey who lives on the hill.
They dined on mince, and slices of quince,
    Which they ate with a runcible spoon;
And hand in hand, on the edge of the sand,
    They danced by the light of the moon,
      The moon,
      The moon,
    They danced by the light of the moon.

Edward Lear

COWS

Half the time they munched the grass, and all the time they lay
Down in the water-meadows, the lazy month of May,
    A-chewing,
    A-mooing,
To pass the hours away.

"Nice weather," said the brown cow.
    "Ah," said the white.
"Grass is very tasty."
    "Grass is all right."

Half the time they munched the grass, and all the time they lay
Down in the water-meadows, the lazy month of May,

A-chewing,
A-mooing,
To pass the hours away.

"Rain coming," said the brown cow.
  "Ah," said the white.
"Flies is very tiresome."
  "Flies bite."

Half the time they munched the grass, and all the time they lay
Down in the water-meadows, the lazy month of May,
    A-chewing,
    A-mooing,
To pass the hours away.

"Time to go," said the brown cow.
  "Ah," said the white.
"Nice chat." "Very pleasant."
  "Night." "Night."

Half the time they munched the grass, and all the time they lay
Down in the water-meadows, the lazy month of May,
    A-chewing,
    A-mooing,
To pass the hours away.

James Reeves

CLOCK-A-CLAY

In the cowslip pips I lie,
Hidden from the buzzing fly,
While green grass beneath me lies,
Pearled with dew like fishes' eyes,
Here I lie, a clock-a-clay,
Waiting for the time of day.

While grassy forest quakes surprise,
And the wild wind sobs and sighs,
My gold home rocks as like to fall,
On its pillar green and tall;
When the pattering rain drives by
Clock-a-clay keeps warm and dry.

Day by day and night by night,
All the week I hide from sight;
In the cowslip pips I lie,
In rain and dew still warm and dry;
Day and night, and night and day,
Red, black-spotted clock-a-clay.

My home shakes in wind and showers,
Pale green pillar topped with flowers,
Bending at the wild wind's breath,
Till I touch the grass beneath;
Here I live, lone clock-a-clay,
Watching for the time of day.

John Clare

NICHOLAS NYE

Thistle and darnel and dock grew there,
  And a bush, in a corner, of may;
On the orchard wall I used to sprawl
  In the blazing heat of the day;
Half asleep and half awake,
  While the birds went twittering by,
And nobody there my lone to share
  But Nicholas Nye.

Nicholas Nye was lean and grey,
  Lame of a leg and old,
More than a score of donkey's years
  He had seen since he was foaled;
He munched the thistles, purple and spiked,
  Would sometimes stop and sigh,
And turn his head, as if he said,
  "Poor Nicholas Nye!"

Alone with his shadow he'd drowse in the meadow,
  Lazily swinging his tail;
At break of day he used to bray, –
  Not much too hearty and hale.
But a wonderful gumption was under his skin,
  And a clear calm light in his eye,
And once in a while he would smile a smile
  Would Nicholas Nye.

Seem to be smiling at me, he would,
From his bush, in the corner, of may –
Bony and ownerless, widowed and worn,
  Knobble-kneed, lonely and grey;
And over the grass would seem to pass
  'Neath the deep dark blue of the sky,
Something much better than words between me
  And Nicholas Nye.

But dusk would come in the apple boughs,
  The green of the glow-worm shine,
The birds in nest would crouch to rest,
  And home I'd trudge to mine;

And there, in the moonlight, dark with dew,
  Asking not wherefore nor why,
Would brood like a ghost, and as still as a post,
  Old Nicholas Nye.
                                    Walter de la Mare

EPITAPH ON A HARE

Here lies, whom hound did ne'er pursue,
  Nor swifter greyhound follow,
Whose foot ne'er tainted morning dew,
  Nor ear heard huntsman's hallo',

Old Tiney, surliest of his kind,
  Who, nursed with tender care,
And to domestic bounds confined,
  Was still a wild Jack-hare.

Though duly from my hand he took
  His pittance every night,
He did it with a jealous look,
  And, when he could, would bite.

His diet was of wheaten bread,
  And milk, and oats, and straw,
Thistles, or lettuces instead,
  With sand to scour his maw.

On twigs of hawthorn he regaled,
  On pippins' russet peel;
And, when his juicy salads failed,
  Sliced carrot pleased him well.

A Turkey carpet was his lawn,
  Whereon he loved to bound,
To skip and gambol like a fawn,
  And swing his rump around.

His frisking was at evening hours,
　　For then he lost his fear;
But most before approaching showers,
　　Or when a storm drew near.

Eight years and five round-rolling moons
　　He thus saw steal away,
Dozing out all his idle noons,
　　And every night at play.

I kept him for his humour's sake,
　　For he would oft beguile
My heart of thoughts that made it ache,
　　And force me to a smile.

But now, beneath this walnut-shade,
　　He finds his long, last home,
And waits, in snug concealment laid,
　　Till gentler Puss shall come.

He, still more aged, feels the shocks
　　From which no care can save,
And, partner once of Tiney's box,
　　Must soon partake his grave.
　　　　　　　　　　William Cowper

The Dog will come when he is called,
　　The Cat will walk away.
The Monkey's cheek is very bald,
　　The Goat is fond of play.
The Parrot is a prate-apace,
　　Yet I know not what he says,
The noble Horse will win the race
　　Or draw you in a chaise.

The Pig is not a feeder nice,
　　The Squirrel loves a nut,
The Wolf would eat you in a trice,
　　The Buzzard's eyes are shut.
The Lark sings high up in the air,
The Linnet in the tree;
The Swan he has a bosom fair,
　　And who so proud as he?
　　　　　　　　　　Adelaide O'Keefe

A centipede was happy quite,
  Until a frog in fun
Said, "Pray, which leg comes after which?"
This raised her mind to such a pitch,
She lay distracted in the ditch
  Considering how to run.

Anon

THE SNAIL

At sunset, when the night-dews fall,
Out of the ivy on the wall
With horns outstretched and pointed tail
Comes the grey and noiseless snail.
On ivy stems she clambers down,
Carrying her house of brown.
Safe in the dark, no greedy eye
Can her tender body spy,
While she herself, a hungry thief,
Searches out the freshest leaf.
She travels on as best she can
Like a toppling caravan.

James Reeves

THE MAGNIFYING GLASS

With this round glass
I can make *Magic* talk –
A myriad shells show
In a scrap of chalk;

Of but an inch of moss
A forest – flowers and trees;
A drop of water
Like a hive of bees.

I lie in wait and watch
How the deft spider jets
The woven web-silk
From his spinnerets;

The tigerish claws he has!
And oh! the silly flies
That stumble into his net –
With all those eyes!

Not even the tiniest thing
But this my glass
Will make more marvellous
And itself surpass.

Yes, and with lenses like it,
Eyeing the moon,
'Twould seem you'd walk there
In an afternoon!

Walter de la Mare

THE FALLOW DEER AT THE LONELY HOUSE

One without looks in tonight
Through the curtain-chink
From the sheet of glistening white;
One without looks in tonight
As we sit and think
By the fender-brink.

We do not discern those eyes
Watching in the snow;
Lit by lamps of rosy dyes
We do not discern those eyes
Wondering, aglow,
Fourfooted, tiptoe.

Thomas Hardy

THE WALRUS AND THE CARPENTER

The sun was shining on the sea,
  Shining with all his might:
He did his very best to make
  The billows smooth and bright –
And this was odd, because it was
  The middle of the night.

The moon was shining sulkily,
  Because she thought the sun
Had got no business to be there
  After the day was done –
"It's very rude of him," she said,
  "To come and spoil the fun!"

The sea was wet as wet could be,
  The sands were dry as dry.
You could not see a cloud, because
  No cloud was in the sky:
No birds were flying overhead –
  There were no birds to fly.

The Walrus and the Carpenter
  Were walking close at hand:
They wept like anything to see
  Such quantities of sand:
"If this were only cleared away,"
  They said, "it *would* be grand!"

"If seven maids with seven mops
    Swept it for half a year,
Do you suppose," the Walrus said,
    "That they could get it clear?"
"I doubt it," said the Carpenter,
    And shed a bitter tear.

"O Oysters, come and walk with us!"
    The Walrus did beseech.
"A pleasant walk, a pleasant talk,
    Along the briny beach:
We cannot do with more than four,
    To give a hand to each."

The eldest Oyster looked at him,
    But never a word he said:
The eldest Oyster winked his eye,
    And shook his heavy head –
Meaning to say he did not choose
    To leave the oyster-bed.

But four young Oysters hurried up,
    All eager for the treat:
Their coats were brushed, their faces washed,
    Their shoes were clean and neat –
And this was odd, because, you know,
    They hadn't any feet.

Four other Oysters followed them,
    And yet another four;
And thick and fast they came at last,
    And more, and more, and more –
All hopping through the frothy waves,
    And scrambling to the shore.

The Walrus and the Carpenter
    Walked on a mile or so,
And then they rested on a rock
    Conveniently low:
And all the little Oysters stood
    And waited in a row.

"The time has come," the Walrus said,
  "To talk of many things:
Of shoes – and ships – and sealing wax –
  Of cabbages – and kings –
And why the sea is boiling hot –
  And whether pigs have wings."

"But wait a bit," the Oysters cried,
  "Before we have our chat;
For some of us are out of breath,
  And all of us are fat!"
"No hurry!" said the Carpenter.
  They thanked him much for that.

"A loaf of bread," the Walrus said,
  "Is what we chiefly need:
Pepper and vinegar besides
  Are very good indeed –
Now, if you're ready, Oysters dear,
  We can begin to feed."

"But not on us!" the Oysters cried,
  Turning a little blue.
"After such kindness, that would be
  A dismal thing to do!"
"The night is fine," the Walrus said.
  "Do you admire the view?

"It was so kind of you to come!
  And you are very nice!"
The Carpenter said nothing but
  "Cut us another slice.
I wish you were not quite so deaf –
  I've had to ask you twice!"

"It seems a shame," the Walrus said,
  "To play them such a trick.
After we've brought them out so far,
  And made them trot so quick!"
The Carpenter said nothing but
  "The butter's spread too thick!"

"I weep for you," the Walrus said:
  "I deeply sympathize."
With sobs and tears he sorted out
  Those of the largest size,
Holding his pocket-handkerchief
  Before his streaming eyes.

"O Oysters," said the Carpenter,
  "You've had a pleasant run!
Shall we be trotting home again?"
  But answer came there none –
And this was scarcely odd, because
  They'd eaten every one.
                    Lewis Carroll

WE'LL LET EACH OTHER ALONE

THE FLY

Little Fly,
Thy summer's play
My thoughtless hand
Has brushed away.

Am not I
A fly like thee?
Or art not thou
A man like me?

For I dance,
And drink, and sing,
Till some blind hand
Shall brush my wing.

If thought is life
And strength and breath,
And the want
Of thought is death;

Then am I
A happy fly,
If I live
Or if I die.

William Blake

THE SNARE

I hear a sudden cry of pain!
    There is a rabbit in a snare:
Now I hear the cry again,
    But I cannot tell from where.

But I cannot tell from where
    He is calling out for aid;
Crying on the frightened air,
    Making everything afraid,

Making everything afraid
   Wrinkling up his little face,
As he cries again for aid;
   – And I cannot find the place!

And I cannot find the place
   Where his paw is in the snare;
Little one! Oh, little one!
   I am searching everywhere!
                    James Stephens

TO A SQUIRREL AT KYLE-NA-NO

Come play with me;
Why should you run
Through the shaking tree
As though I'd a gun
To strike you dead?
When all I would do
Is to scratch your head
And let you go.
                    W. B. Yeats

DONE FOR

Old Ben Bailey
He's been and done
For a small brown bunny
With his long gun.

Glazed are the eyes
That stared so clear,
And no sound stirs
In that hairy ear.

What was once beautiful
Now breathes not,
Bound for Ben Bailey's
Smoking pot.
                    Walter de la Mare

Hopping frog, hop here and be seen,
  I'll not pelt you with stick or stone:
Your cap is laced and your coat is green;
  Goodbye, we'll let each other alone.
                    Christina Rossetti

O'ER VALES AND HILLS

SONG

The feathers of the willow
Are half of them grown yellow
   Above the swelling stream;
And ragged are the bushes,
And rusty now the rushes,
   And wild the clouded gleam.

The thistle now is older,
His stalk begins to moulder,
His head is white as snow;
The branches all are barer,
The linnet's song is rarer,
   The robin pipeth now.
                     Richard Watson Dixon

THE BROOK

I come from haunts of coot and hern,
   I make a sudden sally,
And sparkle out among the fern,
   To bicker down a valley.

By thirty hills I hurry down,
   Or slip between the ridges,
By twenty thorps, a little town,
   And half a hundred bridges.

Till last by Philip's farm I flow
   To join the brimming river,
For men may come and men may go,
   But I go on for ever.

I chatter over stony ways,
   In little sharps and trebles,
I bubble into eddying bays,
   I babble on the pebbles.

With many a curve my banks I fret
   By many a field and fallow,
And many a fairy foreland set
   With willow-weed and mallow.

I chatter, chatter, as I flow
  To join the brimming river,
For men may come and men may go,
  But I go on for ever.

I wind about, and in and out,
  With here a blossom sailing,
And here and there a lusty trout,
  And here and there a grayling.

And here and there a foamy flake
  Upon me, as I travel
With many a silvery waterbreak
  Above the golden gravel,

And draw them all along, and flow
  To join the brimming river,
For men may come and men may go,
  But I go on for ever.

I steal by lawns and grassy plots,
  I slide by hazel covers;
I move the sweet forget-me-nots
  That grow for happy lovers.

I slip, I slide, I gloom, I glance,
  Among my skimming swallows;
I make the netted sunbeam dance
  Against my sandy shallows.

I murmur under moon and stars
  In brambly wildernesses;
I linger by my shingly bars;
  I loiter round my cresses;

And out again I curve and flow
  To join the brimming river,
For men may come and men may go,
  But I go on for ever.

Alfred, Lord Tennyson

THE TIDE IN THE RIVER

The tide in the river,
The tide in the river,
The tide in the river runs deep,
I saw a shiver
Pass over the river
As the tide turned in its sleep.
Eleanor Farjeon

LOVELIEST OF TREES

Loveliest of trees, the cherry now
Is hung with bloom along the bough,
And stands about the woodland ride
Wearing white for Eastertide.

Now, of my threescore years and ten,
Twenty will not come again,
And take from seventy springs a score,
It only leaves me fifty more.

And since to look at things in bloom
Fifty springs are little room,
About the woodlands I will go
To see the cherry hung with snow.
A. E. Housman

IMMALEE

I gather thyme upon the sunny hills,
  And its pure fragrance ever gladdens me,
  And in my mind having tranquillity
I smile to see how my green basket fills.
And by clear streams I gather daffodils;
  And in dim woods find out the cherry-tree,
  And take its fruit and the wild strawberry
And nuts and honey; and live free from ills.
I dwell on the green earth, 'neath the blue sky,
  Birds are my friends, and leaves my rustling roof:
The deer are not afraid of me, and I
  Hear the wild goat, and hail its hastening hoof;
The squirrels sit perked as I pass them by,
  And even the watchful hare stands not aloof.
Christina Rossetti

136

I wandered lonely as a cloud
That floats on high o'er vales and hills,
When all at once I saw a crowd,
A host, of golden daffodils;
Beside the lake, beneath the trees,
Fluttering and dancing in the breeze.

Continuous as the stars that shine
And twinkle on the milky way,
They stretched in never-ending line
Along the margin of a bay:
Ten thousand saw I at a glance,
Tossing their heads in sprightly dance.

The waves beside them danced; but they
Out-did the sparkling waves in glee:
A poet could not but be gay,
In such a jocund company:
I gazed – and gazed – but little thought
What wealth the show to me had brought:

For oft, when on my couch I lie
In vacant or in pensive mood,
They flash upon that inward eye
Which is the bliss of solitude;
And then my heart with pleasure fills,
And dances with the daffodils.
William Wordsworth

THE COUNTRY BEDROOM

My room's a square and candle-lighted boat,
In the surrounding depths of night afloat.
My windows are the portholes, and the seas
The sound of rain on the dark apple-trees.

Sea monster-like beneath, an old horse blows
A snort of darkness from his sleeping nose,
Below, among drowned daisies. Far off, hark!
Far off one owl amidst the waves of dark.
Frances Cornford

A BOY'S SONG

Where the pools are bright and deep,
Where the grey trout lies asleep,
Up the river and over the lea,
That's the way for Billy and me.

Where the blackbird sings the latest,
Where the hawthorn blooms the sweetest,
Where the nestlings chirp and flee,
That's the way for Billy and me.

Where the mowers mow the cleanest,
Where the hay lies thick and greenest,
There to track the homeward bee,
That's the way for Billy and me.

Where the hazel bank is steepest,
Where the shadow falls the deepest,
Where the clustering nuts fall free,
That's the way for Billy and me.

Why the boys should drive away
Little sweet maidens from their play,
Or love to banter and fight so well,
That's the thing I never could tell.

But this I know, I love to play
Through the meadow among the hay;
Up the water, and over the lea,
That's the way for Billy and me.

James Hogg

SLOWLY

Slowly the tide creeps up the sand,
Slowly the shadows cross the land.
Slowly the cart-horse pulls his mile,
Slowly the old man mounts the stile.

Slowly the hands move round the clock,
Slowly the dew dries on the dock.
Slow is the snail – but slowest of all
The green moss spreads on the old brick wall.

James Reeves

THE LONELY SCARECROW

My poor old bones – I've only two –
A broomshank and a broken stave,
My ragged gloves are a disgrace,
My one peg-foot is in the grave.

I wear the labourer's old clothes;
Coat, shirt and trousers all undone.
I bear my cross upon a hill
In rain and shine, in snow and sun.

I cannot help the way I look.
My funny hat is full of hay.
– O, wild birds, come and nest in me!
Why do you always fly away?
James Kirkup

HERE'S TO THEE

Here's to thee,
Old apple-tree!
Stand fast root,
Bear well top,
Pray God send us
A youling crop!

Every twig
Apple big;
Every bough
Apple enow;
Hats full, caps full,
Fill quarter sacks full!
Holla, boys, holla!
Huzza!
Anon

MIDNIGHT

Midnight's bell goes ting, ting, ting, ting, ting,
Then dogs do howl, and not a bird does sing
But the nightingale, and she cries twit, twit, twit:
Owls then on every bough do sit;
Ravens croak on chimney's tops;
The cricket in the chamber hops,
    And the cats cry mew, mew, mew;
The nibbling mouse is not asleep,
But he goes peep, peep, peep, peep, peep,
    And the cats cry mew, mew, mew,
    And still the cats cry mew, mew, mew.
                        Thomas Middleton

HUNTING SONG

Up, up! ye dames, and lasses gay!
To the meadows trip away.
'Tis you must tend the flocks this morn,
And scare the small birds from the corn.
    Not a soul at home may stay:
        For the shepherds must go
        With lance and bow
    To hunt the wolf in the woods today.

Leave the hearth and leave the house
To the cricket and the mouse:
Find grannam out a sunny seat,
With babe and lambkin at her feet.
    Not a soul at home may stay:
        For the shepherds must go
        With lance and bow
    To hunt the wolf in the woods today.
                        Samuel Taylor Coleridge

ADLESTROP

Yes. I remember Adlestrop –
The name, because one afternoon
Of heat the express-train drew up there
Unwontedly. It was late June.

The steam hissed. Someone cleared his throat.
No one left and no one came
On the bare platform. What I saw
Was Adlestrop – only the name

And willows, willow-herb, and grass,
And meadowsweet, and haycocks dry,
No whit less still and lonely fair
Than the high cloudlets in the sky.

And for that minute a blackbird sang
Close by, and round him, mistier,
Farther and farther, all the birds
Of Oxfordshire and Gloucestershire.

Edward Thomas

My heart's in the Highlands, my heart is not here;
My heart's in the Highlands a–chasing the deer;
Chasing the wild deer, and following the roe,
My heart's in the Highlands wherever I go.
Farewell to the Highlands, farewell to the North,
The birth-place of valour, the country of worth;
Wherever I wander, wherever I rove,
The hills of the Highlands for ever I love.

Farewell to the mountains, high covered with snow;
Farewell to the straths and green valleys below;
Farewell to the forests and wild-hanging woods;
Farewell to the torrents and loud-pouring floods.
My heart's in the Highlands, my heart is not here;
My heart's in the Highlands a–chasing the deer;
Chasing the wild deer, and following the roe,
My heart's in the Highlands, wherever I go.

Robert Burns

VICTORIA

From Victoria I can go
To Pevensey Level and Piddinghoe,
Open Winkins and Didling Hill,
Three Cups Corner and Selsey Bill.
I'm the happiest one in all the nation
When my train runs out of Victoria Station.

But O the day when I come to town
From Ditchling Beacon and Duncton Down,
Bramber Castle and Wisborough Green,
Cissbury Ring and Ovingdean!
I'm the sorriest one in all the nation
When my train runs into Victoria Station.

Eleanor Farjeon

SONG

The splendour falls on castle walls
   And snowy summits old in story:
The long light shakes across the lakes,
   And the wild cataract leaps in glory.
Blow, bugle, blow, set the wild echoes flying,
Blow, bugle; answer, echoes, dying, dying, dying.

O hark, O hear! how thin and clear,
   And thinner, clearer, farther going!
O sweet and far from cliff and scar
   The horns of Elfland faintly blowing!
Blow, let us hear the purple glens replying:
Blow, bugle; answer, echoes, dying, dying, dying.

O love, they die in yon rich sky,
   They faint on hill or field or river:
Our echoes roll from soul to soul,
   And grow for ever and for ever.
Blow, bugle, blow, set the wild echoes flying,
And answer, echoes, answer, dying, dying, dying.

Alfred, Lord Tennyson

A CHIP HAT HAD SHE ON

God made the bees,
     And the bees make honey.
The miller's man does all the work,
     But the miller makes the money.
                                        Anon

SILLY SALLIE

Silly Sallie! Silly Sallie!
Called the boys down Blind Man's Alley;
But she, still smiling, never made
A sign she had heard, or answer gave;
Her blue eyes in her skimpy hair
Seemed not to notice they were there;
Seemed still to be watching, rain or shine,
Some other place, not out, but in:
Though it pleased the boys in Blind Man's Alley
Still to be shouting *Silly Sallie!*
                                        Walter de la Mare

SEUMAS BEG

A man was sitting underneath a tree
Outside the village; and he asked me what
Name was upon this place; and said that he
Was never here before—He told a lot

Of stories to me too. His nose was flat!
I asked him how it happened, and he said
—The first mate of the *Mary Anne* did that
With a marling-spike one day—but he was dead,

And jolly good job too; and he'd have gone
A long way to have killed him—Oh, he had
A gold ring in one ear; the other one
—"Was bit off by a crocodile, bedad!"

That's what he said. He taught me how to chew!
He was a real nice man. He liked me too!
                                        James Stephens

WHO'S IN?

"The door is shut fast
   And everyone's out."
But people don't know
   What they're talking about!
Say the fly on the wall,
And the flame on the coals,
And the dog on his rug,
And the mice in their holes,
And the kitten curled up,
And the spiders that spin –
"What, everyone out?
Why, everyone's in!"

Elizabeth Fleming

THEY THAT WASH ON MONDAY

They that wash on Monday
   Have all the week to dry;
They that wash on Tuesday
   Are not so much awry;
They that wash on Wednesday
   Are not so much to blame;
They that wash on Thursday
   Wash for shame;
They that wash on Friday
   Wash in need;
And they that wash on Saturday—
   Oh! They're sluts indeed.

Anon

THE PEDLAR'S CARAVAN

I wish I lived in a caravan,
With a horse to drive, like a pedlar-man!
Where he comes from nobody knows,
Or where he goes to, but on he goes!

His caravan has windows two,
And a chimney of tin, that the smoke comes through;
He has a wife, with a baby brown,
And they go riding from town to town.

Chairs to mend, and delf to sell!
He clashes the basins like a bell;
Tea-trays, baskets ranged in order,
Plates, with alphabets round the border!

The roads are brown, and the sea is green,
But his house is like a bathing-machine;
The world is round, and he can ride,
Rumble and slash, to the other side!

With the pedlar-man I should like to roam,
And write a book when I came home;
All the people would read my book,
Just like the Travels of Captain Cook!
                              William Brighty Rands

As I was going by Charing Cross,
I saw a black man upon a black horse;
They told me it was King Charles the First –
Oh dear, my heart was ready to burst!
                              Anon

THE SOLITARY REAPER

Behold her, single in the field,
Yon solitary Highland Lass!
Reaping and singing by herself;
Stop here, or gently pass!
Alone she cuts and binds the grain,
And sings a melancholy strain;
O listen! for the Vale profound
Is overflowing with the sound.

No Nightingale did ever chaunt
More welcome notes to weary bands
Of travellers in some shady haunt,
Among Arabian sands:
A voice so thrilling ne'er was heard
In spring-time from the Cuckoo-bird.
Breaking the silence of the seas
Among the farthest Hebrides.

Will no one tell me what she sings? –
Perhaps the plaintive numbers flow
For old, unhappy, far-off things,
And battles long ago:
Or is it some more humble lay,
Familiar matter of to-day?
Some natural sorrow, loss, or pain,
That has been, and may be again?

Whate'er the theme, the Maiden sang
As if her song could have no ending;
I saw her singing at her work,
And o'er the sickle bending; –
I listened, motionless and still;
And, as I mounted up the hill,
The music in my heart I bore,
Long after it was heard no more.
William Wordsworth

OLD JACK NOMAN

At mid-day then along the lane
Old Jack Noman appeared again,
Jaunty and old, crooked and tall,
And stopped and grinned at me over the wall,
With a cowslip bunch in his button-hole
And one in his cap. Who could say if his roll
Came from flints in the road, the weather, or ale?
He was welcome as the nightingale.
Not an hour of the sun had been wasted on Jack.
"I've got my Indian complexion back,"
Said he. He was tanned like a harvester,
Like his short clay pipe, like the leaf and bur
That clung to his coat from last night's bed,
Like the ploughland crumbling red.
Fairer flowers were none on the earth
Than his cowslips wet with the dew of their birth,
Or fresher leaves than the cress in his basket.
"Where did they come from, Jack?" "Don't ask it,
And you'll be told no lies." "Very well:
Then I can't buy." "I don't want to sell.
Take them and these flowers, too, free.

Perhaps you have something to give me?
Wait till next time. The better the day . . .
The Lord couldn't make a better, I say;
If he could, he never has done."
So off went Jack with his roll–walk–run,
Leaving his cresses from Oakshott rill
And his cowslips from Wheatham hill.

Edward Thomas

A STRANGE MEETING

The moon is full, and so am I;
   The night is late, the ale was good;
And I must go two miles and more
   Along a country road.

Now what is this that's drawing near?
   It seems a man, and tall;
But where the face should show its white
   I see no white at all.

Where is his face: or do I see
   The back part of his head,
And, with his face turned round about,
   He walks this way? I said.

He's close at hand, but where's the face?
   What devil is this I see?
I'm glad my body's warm with ale,
   There's trouble here for me.

I clutch my staff, I make a halt,
   "His blood or mine," said I.
"Good-night," the black man said to me,
   As he went passing by.

W. H. Davies

MEG MERRILEES

Old Meg she was a Gipsy,
   And liv'd upon the Moors:
Her bed it was the brown heath turf,
   And her house was out of doors.

Her apples were swart blackberries,
   Her currants pods o' broom;
Her wine was dew o' the wild white rose,
   Her book a churchyard tomb.

Her Brothers were the craggy hills,
   Her Sisters larchen trees—
Alone with her great family
   She liv'd as she did please.

No breakfast had she many a morn,
   No dinner many a noon,
And 'stead of supper she would stare
   Full hard against the Moon.

But every morn of woodbine fresh
　　She made her garlanding,
And every night the dark glen Yew
　　She wove, and she would sing.

And with her fingers old and brown,
　　She plaited Mats o' Rushes,
And gave them to the Cottagers
　　She met among the Bushes.

Old Meg was brave as Margaret Queen
　　And tall as Amazon:
An old red blanket cloak she wore;
　　A chip hat had she on.
God rest her aged bones somewhere –
　　She died full long agone!

John Keats

SIGH AS YOU SING

SONG

Weep, weep, ye woodmen! wail;
　　Your hands with sorrow wring!
Your master Robin Hood lies dead,
　　Therefore sigh as you sing.

Here lies his primer and his beads,
　　His bent bow and his arrows keen,
His good sword and his holy cross.
　　Now cast on flowers fresh and green;

And, as they fall, shed tears and say
　　Well-a, well-a-day! well-a, well-a-day!
Thus cast ye flowers, and sing,
　　And on to Wakefield take your way.

Anthony Munday

THE BONNY EARL OF MORAY

Ye Hielands and ye Lawlands,
　　Oh, where have you been?
They have slain the Earl of Moray,
　　And have laid him on the green!

Oh wae betide thee, Huntly,
　　And wherefore did ye sae?
I bade you bring him wi' you,
　　But forbade you him to slay.

He was a braw gallant,
　　And he rade at the ring;
And the bonny Earl of Moray,
　　He might have been a king!

He was a braw gallant,
　　And he played at the ba';
And the bonny Earl of Moray
　　Was the flower amang them a'.

He was a braw gallant,
　　And he played at the glove;
And the bonny Earl of Moray,
　　Oh he was the Queen's love!

Oh lang, lang will his lady
　　Look frae the Castle Doune,
Ere she see the Earl of Moray
　　Come sounding thro' the town!

Ye Hielands and ye Lawlands,
　　Oh, where have you been?
They have slain the Earl of Moray,
　　And have laid him on the green!

Anon

THE SANDS OF DEE

"O Mary, go and call the cattle home,
  And call the cattle home,
  And call the cattle home,
  Across the sands of Dee."
The western wind was wild and dank with foam,
  And all alone went she.

The western tide crept up along the sand,
  And o'er and o'er the sand,
  And round and round the sand,
  As far as eye could see.
The rolling mist came down and hid the land:
  And never home came she.

"O is it weed, or fish, or floating hair –
  A tress of golden hair,
  A drowned maiden's hair,
  Above the nets at sea?"
Was never salmon yet that shone so fair
  Among the stakes of Dee.

They rowed her in across the rolling foam,
  The cruel crawling foam,
  The cruel hungry foam,
  To her grave beside the sea,
But still the boatmen hear her call the cattle home,
  Across the sands of Dee.

Charles Kingsley

A DIRGE

Call for the robin red-breast and the wren,
Since o'er shady groves they hover,
And with leaves and flowers do cover
The friendless bodies of unburied men.
Call unto his funeral dole
The ant, the field-mouse, and the mole,
To rear him hillocks that shall keep him warm,
And (when gay tombs are robbed) sustain no harm;
But keep the wolf far thence, that's foe to men,
For with his nails he'll dig them up again.

John Webster

PROUD MAISIE

Proud Maisie is in the wood,
    Walking so early;
Sweet Robin sits on the bush,
    Singing so rarely.

"Tell me, thou bonny bird,
    When shall I marry me?"
"When six braw gentlemen
    Kirkward shall carry ye."

"Who makes the bridal bed,
    Birdie, say truly?"
"The grey-headed sexton,
    That delves the grave duly.

"The glow-worm o'er grave and stone
    Shall light thee steady.
The owl from the steeple sing,
    'Welcome, proud lady!' "
                   Sir Walter Scott

EPITAPH ON MARTHA SNELL

Poor Martha Snell has gone away,
She would, if she could, but she couldn't stay,
She had two sore legs and a baddish cough,
But it were her legs that carried her off.
                   Anon

Go and tell Aunt Nancy,
Go and tell Aunt Nancy,
Go and tell Aunt Nancy,
    The old grey goose is dead.

The one that she was saving,
The one that she was saving,
The one that she was saving,
    To make a feather bed.

She died on Friday,
She died on Friday,
She died on Friday,
    Behind the old barn shed.

She left nine little goslings,
She left nine little goslings,
She left nine little goslings,
    To scratch for their own bread.
                   Anon

WITH SWEET-BRIAR AND BON-FIRE

THE GHOST'S SONG

Wae's me! wae's me!
The acorn's not yet
Fallen from the tree
That's to grow the wood,
That's to make the cradle,
That's to rock the bairn,
That's to grow a man,
That's to lay me.

Anon

A man of words and not of deeds
Is like a garden full of weeds;

And when the weeds begin to grow,
It's like a garden full of snow;

And when the snow begins to fall,
It is like birds upon a wall;

And when the birds begin to fly,
It's like a shipwreck in the sky;

And when the sky begins to roar,
It's like a lion at the door;

And when the door begins to crack,
It's like a stick across your back;

And when your back begins to smart,
It's like a penknife in your heart;

And when your heart begins to bleed,
Oh then you're dead and dead indeed!

Anon

And can the physician make sick men well?
And can the magician a fortune divine?
Without lily, germander, and sops-in-wine?
   With sweet-briar
   And bon-fire
   And strawberry wire
   And columbine.

Within and without, in and out, round as a ball,
With hither and thither, as straight as a line,
With lily, germander, and sops-in-wine,
   With sweet-briar
   And bon-fire
   And strawberry wire
   And columbine.

When Saturn did live, there lived no poor,
The king and the beggar with roots did dine,
With lily, germander, and sops-in-wine,
   With sweet-briar
   And bon-fire
   And strawberry wire
   And columbine.

Anon

THIS IS THE KEY

This is the key of the kingdom:
In that kingdom there is a city.
In that city there is a town.
In that town there is a street.
In that street there is a lane.
In that lane there is a yard.
In that yard there is a house.
In that house there is a room.
In that room there is a bed.
On that bed there is a basket.
In that basket there are some flowers.
Flowers in a basket.
Basket on the bed.
Bed in the room.
Room in the house.
House in the yard.
Yard in the lane.
Lane in the street.
Street in the town.
Town in the city.
City in the kingdom.
Of the kingdom this is the key.

Anon

CELANTA AT THE WELL OF LIFE

Gently dip, but not too deep,
For fear you make the golden beard to weep.
Fair maiden, white and red,
Comb me smooth, and stroke my head,
And thou shalt have some cockell-bread.
Gently dip, but not too deep,
For fear thou make the golden beard to weep.
Fair maid, white and red,
Comb me smooth, and stroke my head,
And every hair a sheaf shall be,
And every sheaf a golden tree.

George Peele

ROCK THEM, ROCK THEM, LULLABY

You spotted snakes with double tongue,
  Thorny hedgehogs, be not seen;
Newts and blind-worms, do no wrong,
  Come not near our fairy queen.

  Philomel, with melody
  Sing in our sweet lullaby;
Lulla, lulla, lullaby; lulla, lulla, lullaby:
  Never harm,
  Nor spell nor charm,
Come our lovely lady nigh.
So, good night, with lullaby.

Weaving spiders, come not here;
  Hence, you long-legg'd spinners, hence!
Beetles black, approach not near;
  Worm nor snail, do no offence.

  Philomel, with melody
  Sing in our sweet lullaby;
Lulla, lulla, lullaby; lulla, lulla, lullaby:
  Never harm,
  Nor spell nor charm,
Come our lovely lady nigh.
So, good night, with lullaby.

William Shakespeare

SWEET AND LOW

Sweet and low, sweet and low,
  Wind of the western sea,
Low, low, breathe and blow,
  Wind of the western sea!
Over the rolling waters go,
Come from the dying moon, and blow,
  Blow him again to me;
While my little one, while my pretty one, sleeps.

Sleep and rest, sleep and rest,
　　Father will come to thee soon;
Rest, rest, on mother's breast,
　　Father will come to thee soon;
Father will come to his babe in the nest,
Silver sails all out of the west
　　Under the silver moon:
Sleep, my little one, sleep, my pretty one, sleep.

Alfred, Lord Tennyson

A CRADLE SONG

Golden slumbers kiss your eyes,
Smiles awake you when you rise.
Sleep, pretty wantons, do not cry,
And I will sing a lullaby:
Rock them, rock them, lullaby.

Care is heavy, therefore, sleep you;
You are care, and care must keep you.
Sleep, pretty wantons, do not cry,
And I will sing a lullaby:
Rock them, rock them, lullaby.

Thomas Dekker

Acknowledgements

We wish to thank the following for permission to include copyright poems by:
HILAIRE BELLOC: Gerald Duckworth and Co., Ltd. for *The Yak* from *The Bad Child's Book of Beasts* and *Matilda* from *Cautionary Tales,* and Alfred A. Knopf, Inc. for the same poems from *Cautionary Verses*, copyright 1931 by Hilaire Belloc; FRANCES CORNFORD: The Cresset Press for *The Country Bedroom* from *Collected Poems*, 1954; W. H. DAVIES: Mrs. H. M. Davies and Jonathan Cape, Ltd. for *The Cat* and *A Strange Meeting* from *Collected Poems*, 1942; WALTER DE LA MARE: The Literary Trustees of Walter de la Mare and the Society of Authors for *At the Keyhole, Nicholas Nye, The Magnifying Glass, Done For* and *Silly Sallie*; T. S. ELIOT: Mr. T. S. Eliot and Faber and Faber, Ltd. for *The Song of the Jellicles* from *Old Possum's Book of Practical Cats*, and Harcourt, Brace and World, Inc. for the same poem from their edition of *Old Possum's Book of Practical Cats*, copyright 1939, by T. S. Eliot; ELEANOR FARJEON: Miss Eleanor Farjeon and Michael Joseph, Ltd. for *The Tide in The River* and *Cat!* from *Silver, Sand and Snow*, © 1958, and J. M. Dent and Sons, Ltd. for *Victoria* from *Kings and Queens*, copyright 1953; ELIZABETH FLEMING: Blackie and Son, Ltd. for *Who's In*; COLIN FRANCIS: Constable and Co., Ltd. for *Tony O* from *Come Hither* by Walter de la Mare; ROBERT GRAVES: Mr. Robert Graves and International Authors N.V. for *Warning to Children* from *The Penny Fiddle*, published by Cassell & Co., Ltd. and Doubleday and Co., Inc.; WILFRID GIBSON: the author's representative and Macmillan and Co., Ltd., London for *Flannan Isle* from *Collected Poems 1905-1925*; THOMAS HARDY: the Trustees of the Hardy Estate and Macmillan and Co., Ltd., London for *Weathers* and *The Fallow Deer at the Lonely House* from *The Collected Poems of Thomas Hardy*, and The Macmillan Company, New York, for the same poems from *Collected Poems* by Thomas Hardy, copyright 1925 by The Macmillan Company; A. E. HOUSMAN: the Society of Authors as the literary representative of the Estate of the late A. E. Housman and Jonathan Cape, Ltd. for *Loveliest of Trees* from their edition of *Collected Poems*, and Holt, Rinehart and Winston, Inc. for the same poem taken from their authorised edition of *A Shropshire Lad* in *Complete Poems*, © 1959, by Holt, Rinehart and Winston, Inc.; RUDYARD KIPLING: Mrs. George Bambridge, Macmillan and Co., Ltd., London, the Macmillan Co. of Canada Ltd. and Doubleday and Co., Inc. for *A Smuggler's Song* from *Puck of Pook's Hill*; JAMES KIRKUP: Mr. James Kirkup and Oxford University Press for *The Lonely Scarecrow* from *Refusal to Conform*, © 1963; JOHN MASEFIELD: Dr. John Masefield, O.M. and the Society of Authors for *Posted as Missing*, and The Macmillan Company, New York, for the same poem from their edition of *The Story of a Round Horse*, copyright 1912 by The Macmillan Company (renewed 1940 by John Masefield); HAROLD MONRO: Mrs. Alida Monro for *Milk for the Cat*; JAMES REEVES: Mr. James Reeves, E. P. Dutton and Co., Inc. and William Heinemann, Ltd. for *Slowly* and *The Snail* from *The Wandering Moon*, and Mr. James Reeves, E. P. Dutton and Co., Inc. and Oxford University Press for *Cows* from *The Blackbird in the Lilac*; OSBERT SITWELL: Mr. Osbert Sitwell and Gerald Duckworth and Co., Ltd. for *Winter the Huntsman* from *Selected Poems Old and New*; JAMES STEPHENS: Mrs. Iris Wise and Macmillan and Co., Ltd., London, for *Seumas Beg* and *The Snare* from *Collected Poems*, and The Macmillan Company, New York, for *Seumas Beg* from *Collected Poems*, copyright 1909 by The Macmillan Company, and for *The Snare* from *Collected Poems*, copyright 1915 by The Macmillan Company (copyright 1943 by James Stephens); EDWARD THOMAS: Mrs. Helen Thomas for *Adlestrop*, and Mrs. Thomas and Faber and Faber, Ltd. for *A Cat, If I should ever by chance grow rich* and *Old Jack Noman* (an extract from *May the Twenty-third*) from *Collected Poems*; W. J. TURNER: the Author's Representatives and Sidgwick and Jackson Ltd. for *India* from *The Hunter and Other Poems* by W. J. Turner; WILLIAM WATSON: George G. Harrap and Co., Ltd. for *The Ballad of Semmerwater* from *The Poems of Sir William Watson 1878-1935*; W. B. YEATS: Mrs. W. B. Yeats and The Macmillan Company, New York for *The Song of Wandering Aengus*, copyright 1906 by The Macmillan Company (renewed 1934 by William Butler Yeats) and *To A Squirrel at Kyle-Na-No*, copyright 1919 by The Macmillan Company (renewed 1946 by Bertha Georgie Yeats) from *Collected Poems*, and Macmillan and Co., Ltd., London, for the same poems from their edition of *Collected Poems of W. B. Yeats*.

Index of Authors

Index of First Lines

THE END